nov
1500

BUTLIN: TURNER · WATERCOLOURS

MARTIN BUTLIN

Turner · Watercolours

WATSON-GUPTILL PUBLICATIONS · NEW YORK

PUBLISHED IN THE UNITED STATES OF AMERICA MCMLXV BY WATSON-GUPTILL PUBLICATIONS

NEW YORK, NEW YORK

© MCMLXII BY PHOEBUS-VERLAG, BASEL.

PRINTED IN SWITZERLAND.

LIBRARY OF CONGRESS CATALOG CARD NUMBER 65-23371.

THE WATERCOLOURS of J. M. W. Turner are one of the greatest achievements in the history of English art. Turner's range and technical virtuosity were unsurpassed, and in quality his best work ranks with even the masterpieces of his more single-minded rivals. This achievement is all the more remarkable in that Turner's main interest lay elsewhere, in his oil-paintings.

The vast range of Turner's watercolours, in both style and subject matter, can only be hinted at in this brief anthology of thirty-two plates. The extent of his development, from early topographical works to late visions of colour, was matched by the enormous variety within his work at any one time. Constant activity for the engraver and finished works for sale to individual patrons were supplemented by watercolours painted purely for their own sake, sometimes as records of localities or effects of light and atmosphere, sometimes as experiments in colour. These private watercolours, like the oil-paintings never exhibited in his lifetime, are now the most highly prized of his works, perhaps over much at the expense of the more finished works on which he staked his contemporary reputation. Turner was indeed the first major British artist to show this division between a private and a public art. In addition the circumstances of his time made it possible for him to be dependent, in his public art, not pri-

marily on the commissions of patrons but on deliberate appeals to the public through engravings and works painted for exhibition.

It is therefore at first sight surprising that, in contrast to the large number of watercolours made for engravings, so few were made for exhibition or as sketches for the many exhibited oils. Though Turner's earliest exhibits at the Royal Academy, from 1790 to 1795, were watercolours alone, these were all but absent from the Academy after 1802 except in 1811, though some may have been shown at Turner's own gallery during the first decade or so of the century. The only important exhibitions of his watercolours in subsequent years were those given by his patron Walter Fawkes in 1819 and by the publishers of his engravings in the 1820s and '30s. For most of his career a small number of regular patrons bought his finished watercolours either directly from him or, in his later years, through the dealer Thomas Griffith.

The almost complete absence of direct watercolour sketches for oil-paintings, or indeed for finished watercolours, reflects Turner's ability to work from the slightest of pencil sketches, reinforced by a phenomenal visual memory. The most outstanding example of this is the oil-painting of "Norham Castle" at the Tate Gallery, painted in about 1840–45 on the basis of sketches made over forty years earlier. Even more detailed works were often made on the basis of the merest scribbles. In the majority of cases the original drawing or watercolour served as no more than an *aide-memoire*, the resulting painting being an independently worked-out composition. Such was the case of the two oils of "The Burning of the Houses of Parliament" (see plate 16). Certain of the Venetian oils made after his visit in 1840 are probably the only examples of his taking over complete compositions from watercolour sketches, and in this they differ radically from his first Venetian oils, exhibited in 1833 after what was almost certainly an absence from Venice of nearly fifteen years.

Although Turner's whole practice as an artist depended on his sketching tours, of which he would often make two or three in one year, his exceptional visual memory also meant that very few of even the most spontaneous of his watercolours were actually made on the spot; those of the burning of the Houses of Parliament in 1834 (plate 16) are one of the rare exceptions. He would usually spend his time out of doors filling sketchbooks with pencil drawings, fairly detailed in his earlier years but later more and more sketchy. Back at his lodgings in the evenings he would either colour these sketches direct or make separate watercolours in a larger sketchbook. A contemporary witness gives evidence of this practice in Rome in 1819 (see plate 10) and the sketchbooks, large and small, from this Italian tour illustrate it particularly fully: the Roman scene on plate 10 comes from a sketchbook also containing pencil sketches, some partly finished in watercolour, whereas the Venetian sunrise on plate 9 is from a sketchbook filled solely with sketches in colour, Turner's pencil drawings of Venice having been made in separate smaller books.

Moreover not all of Turner's watercolours were inspired directly by visual observation. Some of the colour sketches made at Venice in 1819 are mere lay-ins without any reference to locality; here Turner began with an idea of colour rather than of a specific scene or place (see plate 9). There are similar examples in other sketchbooks. Even some of his watercolours with definite subjects, such as the so-called "Venice from Fusina" (plate 19), seem to be studies more of an abstract relationship of colours than the direct result of a visual experience. In his later works his use of colour often bore little relation to nature, as in the red cows on plate 32.

Turner's output of oil-paintings was fairly steady from his first exhibit in 1796 to the year before his death in 1851, the only major periods of slackening off being during the four or five years following his first visit to Italy in 1819 and in the late 1840s. On the other hand his activity as a watercolourist seems to have been more sporadic, though the large number of undateable "colour beginnings" and other miscellaneous examples in the Turner Bequest makes this difficult to establish with certainty. Particular tours or patrons seem to have inspired an exceptionally large proportion of his watercolours. Instances are his visits to the Rhine in 1817, to Italy in 1819, 1835 and 1840, and to Switzerland in the early 1840s, and the patronage of Walter Fawkes at Farnley Hall and Lord Egremont at Petworth. Turner's work for engraving also fluctuated in quantity, for more practical reasons. The development of his watercolours, though sometimes influencing that of his oils, was less consistent; it was also more subject to the varied demands of differences in purpose.

Joseph Mallord William Turner was born on the 23rd April 1775, the son of a London barber. His first dated drawings were made in 1786 and 1787 and are mainly copies from engravings. In 1789, when staying with an uncle near Oxford, Turner made what seem to have been his first sketches from nature, and from some of these he painted finished watercolours (see British Museum, Turner Bequest II and III). These seem to mark the beginning of his professional career, his father offering such works for sale at his barber's shop. In December 1789 Turner was entered as a student at the Royal Academy Schools where he continued to attend until 1793, and it was probably during this period that he also studied with the topographical watercolourist Thomas Malton. In addition he worked on his own copying drawings by other artists such as Edward Dayes and, according to Turner's early but unreliable biographer Thornbury, studied architecture with Thomas Hardwick. Turner exhibited one watercolour at the Royal Academy in 1790, two in the next two years and from then on an increasing number until 1796, when he also showed his first oil; subsequently his oil-paintings gradually supplanted his water-colours. His success was rapid: he was elected an Associate of the Royal Academy in 1799 and a full member in 1802.

The watercolours in the Bristol and Malmesbury sketchbook of 1791 are typical of his earliest works, vigorous but coarse in execution, with ill-assimilated conventions such as framing trees and panoramic views seen under hanging branches (see British Museum, Turner Bequest VI and VII). The next year Turner visited Wales, the first of many such tours made with the deliberate intention of accumulating material for topographical works, but it was not until the exhibition of 1794, after a further Welsh trip, that he showed himself fully a master of this idiom in the "Inside of Tintern Abbey, Monmouthshire" (probably Victoria and Albert Museum; a similar watercolour is in the British Museum, Turner Bequest XXIII–A).

In this work, as in a large number of other topographical watercolours executed in the 1790s for exhibition or for engraving, of which "Christ Church from the Meadows" (plate 1) is a fine though late example, Turner perfected the "tinted drawing" of the eighteenth century. The starting point was a detailed pencil drawing and the colouring was carefully controlled to preserve the unity of the design, the main areas of light and shade being laid in with grey washes before the final addition of local colour; the colour was largely restricted to restrained tones of brown and greyish-green and blue. There was no opportunity for improvisation or bravura of handling: in such half-finished works as "The Western Tower, Ely Cathedral", 1794 (British Museum, Turner Bequest XXI-Y), part was left with the pencil outline alone while the rest was completely coloured down to the last detail. But these works are already distinguished from those of Turner's contemporaries by their superior technique and a subtle feeling for light, skilfully used in the composition: for instance in "Christ Church from the Meadows" the college buildings, though relatively distant and small in scale, draw the eye by their lighter, glowing tonality, and the central motif is emphasised by the white of the clouds above and the two figures on the river bank below.

For three years, probably from 1794 to 1797, Turner was employed in the winter evenings by the amateur Dr. Monro, together with a number of other young artists including Thomas Girtin. According to Farington "Girtin drew in outlines and Turner washed in the effects. They were chiefly employed in copying the outlines or unfinished drawings of Cozens, etc., of which copies they made finished drawings". These copies (some of which, by both Turner and other artists, were bought by Turner at Dr. Monro's sale in 1833 and are now in the British Museum, Turner Bequest CCCLXXI to CCCLXXVII) were made after sketches done in Italy and Switzerland in 1782–3 by J. R. Cozens, who became one of the doctor's patients at the Bethlehem

Hospital, Lambeth, in 1794. They introduced Turner not only to a type of landscape drawing completely different from the topographical works of his first masters but also to scenery still more dramatic than that he had seen in Wales; it is noteworthy that on his trip to Switzerland in 1802 he visited and sketched many of the sights already treated by Cozens.

Besides bringing Turner into contact with the works of Cozens and other artists represented in Dr. Monro's collection this employment was particularly important in introducing him to Girtin. Over the next few years the two young artists, both born in the same year, worked together in evolving a new style in which the technique of the topographical tradition was replaced by a much freer method of working directly in watercolour, often exploiting the texture of the paper and such devices as washing-out and scratching-out. Farington's diary records a visit from Turner a few years later, in 1799, when "he told me he has no systematic process for making drawings... By washing and occasionally rubbing out, he at last expresses in some degree the idea in his mind." However, Turner did not abandon all the features of the old tradition. In some of his later topographical works such as "Bolton Abbey", 1809 (plate 4), he retained the degree of detail and some of the pictorial conventions while abandoning the pre-determining of shadows by monochrome washes. Nor were he and Girtin the first artists to dispense with the three stages of pencil drawing, chiaroscuro washes and final tinting. But their revolution, partly through the very fact of being made by skilled practitioners in the tradition, was a fundamental one, making possible a new improvisatory approach and being accompanied by a completely new sense of scale and richness of colour. It is difficult to date this revolution exactly: such a work as "Old London Bridge" of

about 1796–7 (British Museum, Turner Bequest, XXXIII–U) is completely free from the traditional technique and discipline that still underlies "Christ Church from the Meadows" of 1799 (plate 1).

In Turner's case the new approach to watercolour was partly the result of his growing practice in oils, and it was in these that his ambitions were most apparent in the later 1790s and the first years of the nineteenth century. This was the period in which his rivalry with the Old Masters was at its height: from Wilson he turned to Titian, Poussin and Claude in his efforts to emulate the Grand Manner. In his watercolours a similar interest coincided with his discovery of the grandeur of Scottish and Alpine scenery, the first in 1801, the second in 1802 when the Treaty of Amiens brought a truce to the war with France and made it possible for him to go abroad in the steps of J.R. Cozens.

Some of the most impressive results of these journeys are in monochrome. The finished watercolours of the next two years such as "The Source of the Arveyron", exhibited in 1803 (Farnley Hall), and "The Great Fall of the Reichenbach" of 1804 (Bedford), are over-large in scale and heavy in colour. Girtin, who died in 1802, might have been better able to sustain the full implications of the Grand Manner in the medium of watercolour.

It is a relief therefore to turn to the few informal colour sketches made at this time, such as those painted at Edinburgh in 1801 (plate 2), in which he seems to have been content to record a visual impression unaffected by the aspirations to grandeur that inspired his contemporary oils. The delicacy of these sketches, completely different in their technique of broad flat washes from the equally sensitive topographical watercolours of the mid 1790s, looks forward to the atmospheric impressions of Venice painted in 1819 (plate 9).

The contrast of these sketches with the finished Swiss watercolours is typical of the way in which Turner developed different styles for different purposes; at the same time his topographical works, such as those painted for the *Oxford Almanac* up to 1811 or of the neighbourhood of Farnley Hall from 1809 to 1819 (plate 4), continued though in a modified form the tradition of his earliest works. This variation of style according to the purpose of each type of work reflected Turner's acceptance of the academic hierarchy of genres, each having its own appropriate treatment; in this hierarchy ordinary landscape held a low place. Turner's interest in "elevated" subjects for his oil-paintings, particularly classical and historical ones, was a symptom of this attitude, as was his attempt to raise the status of at least some of his watercolours by a grandeur of subject and treatment. His conscious division of his work into different categories is most apparent in the plan of his *Liber Studiorum*, which was evolved in 1806 and appeared in instalments until the project finally petered out in 1819. This was a series of engravings, based on sepia drawings, in which Turner displayed the variety of different landscape conventions at his command, dividing them into categories such as "History, Mountains, Pastoral, Marine and Architecture", together with one abbreviated to "E.P.", probably "Epic Pastoral".

By the middle of the decade Turner was better able to combine something of the dignity and power of the Grand Manner with the scale and intimacy appropriate to watercolour, as in some sketches made on the Thames in about 1806 (plate 3). These sketches also contain the germs of one of the most marked revolutions in the development of Turner's style, in which he turned away from the Grand Manner to the depiction of the English landscape under varying conditions of light and atmosphere, and in which he revealed, at first unconsciously, his dissatisfaction with the academic hierarchy of genres. A return to English subjects was a feature of some of the oil-paintings exhibited in 1806 and 1807 but these, like this group of watercolours, were still strongly influenced by Claude and Poussin in composition and were relatively dry and unatmospheric. One of the works exhibited the following year, "The Union of the Thames and Isis" (Tate Gallery), shows a marked development in naturalism, but the change was only fully apparent in a whole group of oils shown in 1809. The direct cause of this development can be seen in another set of Thames sketches, almost certainly made in 1807, but these are not watercolours but oils, on small veneer panels and perhaps the only oils Turner painted in the open air. Though there are some contemporary watercolours that show a new freshness and directness akin to the oil sketches (British Museum, Turner Bequest xcv), it is significant that Turner achieved this revolution in the medium of oil-painting.

During the next ten years this return to nature reached perhaps its peak in some sky studies that rival those of Constable (plate 7), but in finished watercolours Turner was largely marking time. The results however are among the most serenely lovely of his works, as can be seen from plate 4, an early example of the most important group of watercolours painted during this period, the views of Wharfedale in the neighbourhood of his friend and patron Walter Fawkes of Farnley Hall. In 1815 the end of the Napoleonic wars made it once again possible to visit Europe, but Turner was by now so busy with his work for the engravers that he could not get away until the late summer of 1817, when he paid a brief but very productive visit to the Low Countries and the Rhine between Cologne and Mainz. The watercolours resulting from this trip are masterpieces of technical virtuosity and sensitivity to effects of light but they represent the culmination of the first half of Turner's career rather than any new departure (plates 5 and 6); in much the same way the oil-paintings exhibited in 1818 and 1819, "The Dort", "Raby Castle" and "Richmond Hill" (Farnley Hall; Baltimore; Tate Gallery) consolidate the achievements of the preceding years.

At last, in 1819, came Turner's first visit to Italy. Such a trip was inevitable, in view of the nature of the aspirations revealed in the large historical compositions and Claudian landscapes which, notwithstanding the renewed naturalism based on his Thames sketches of 1806–7, had formed a large proportion of his exhibits at the Royal Academy since the beginning of the century. The visit had been anticipated even in his watercolours: in 1818 and earlier in 1819 Turner had painted, for engravings, two views of Vesuvius and one of Venice from drawings by other artists. The impact of Italy was none the less overwhelming. The effect on Turner's oils was in fact only too great, resulting in what Ruskin termed "nonsense pictures", packed with exquisite but unassimilated incidents each one of which would make a small masterpiece on its own; after the first of these, "Rome from the Vatican" (Tate Gallery), was exhibited in 1820 Turner himself seems to have recoiled, exhibiting only three oils in the next five years. The finished watercolours that resulted from the visit, with their detail and bright colour, are also rather disappointing.

The watercolour sketches actually painted in Italy are another matter. "The Nymphæum of Alexander Severus" (plate 10) is still fairly close to the Rhine watercolours of two years earlier, though the effect of Rome with its architecture and traditions is seen in a new monumentality and sense of scale, but in other examples, particularly those of Venice such as "San Giorgio from the Dogana" (plate 9), a new world of light and colour is revealed. The seeds of this revolution lay in much earlier works but it required the vision of the Venetian lagoon under the morning sun to fuse the simple means and depiction of atmosphere of "Edinburgh from the West" (plate 2) with the heightened tonality of "Bolton Abbey" (plate 4) in this joyous expression of the life-enhancing forces of nature.

The effect of Turner's new use of thin transparent washes over white paper is seen even in some of his topographical works of the next decade, for example "Whitby" (plate 13): the luminosity of the small port nestling in the bay in the middle distance would have been impossible earlier. But of the two qualities now fully liberated by the Italian journey, light and colour, Turner seems in the 1820s and earlier 1830s to have turned more to colour, and a complete balance between the two did not appear until the 1840s. For, unlike "Whitby", a large number of his watercolours of this period were done in opaque body-colour on blue paper, a technique that stresses above all else strong, unmodulated colours. These include the miraculous group of indoor and outdoor sketches done at Petworth in about 1830 (plates 14 and 15) and the topographical views painted for the *Rivers of France* engravings between 1825 and 1835 (plate 12). The last, being for reproduction in black and white, can only have been executed in such a medium because Turner wished to explore its potentialities to the full, though their detailed finish in comparison with the Petworth works shows some concession to their purpose. This time Turner's watercolours were in advance of his oils, these works anticipating a similar interest in strong, glowing colours to be seen in Turner's oil-paintings of a few years later, particularly in such figure-scenes as "Pilate washing his Hands", exhibited in 1830, and the unexhibited "The Letter" of about five years later; "Interior at Petworth", painted perhaps in 1837, was the climax of this development (all these paintings are in the Tate Gallery).

But already by the mid 1830s, in a group of watercolours painted at Venice (see plates 17 and 18), Turner had begun to reintroduce into his works in body-colour a much greater feeling of atmosphere, using more brokenly applied colours on paper of a shade which blended with rather than contrasted with them. One reason for this development may have been the rekindling of Turner's interest in night scenes characterised by special effects of light, particularly fire, on the occasion of the spectacular burning down of the Houses of Parliament one night in October 1834. The watercolour sketches made on the spot (plate 16) show Turner's spontaneous mastery of ordinary watercolour on white paper, but for the more deliberate Venetian night scenes of, almost certainly, the following year he returned to using body-colour, this time on a brown paper which supplied a suitable darkish tone, enriching and adding subtlety to the colouring and unifying the composition.

Turner painted a number of other works in body-colour on tinted paper during this stay in Venice – exciting interiors of theatres and wine-shops with glistening reflections on gilt and glass, and peaceful canal and lagoon scenes (plate 18), some of them on grey rather than on brown paper – but after 1835 he seems to have largely abandoned this technique. "A Gurnard" of about 1839 (plate 23) shows it in its last, most ethereal phase. Other works almost certainly painted at Venice in 1835 show him exploring the full possibilities of ordinary watercolour on white paper, ranging from the heavily saturated tones of "Venice from Fusina" (plate 19) to the expressive vigour of thin washes, assisted by scratching and damping out, depicting a

"Storm at Venice" (plate 20); in this last Turner used drawing with pen or the point of the brush to suggest architectural detail in a way that became increasingly common among his late works, both in oil and watercolour.

The fires and storms found in some of the Venetian works of 1835 are part of a theme that was becoming more and more the real subject of Turner's oil-paintings at this time, the overwhelming strength of the forces of nature. From as early as the first decade of the century Turner had often chosen subjects of storm, fire or avalanche and in 1819 he had gone specially from Rome to see an eruption of Vesuvius, but by the 1830s he was beginning to express the superiority of these forces over the puniness of material objects more openly, through such purely visual means as the blurring of the distinctions between the forces and the supposedly solid forms on which they impinged. In "Staffa, Fingal's Cave" for example, an oil-painting exhibited in 1832 (the Hon. Gavin Astor), sea and cliffs are swept together in energetic repeated brush-strokes which ignore their separate entities. This development culminated in the great vortex-like compositions of the 1840s such as "Snow-Storm, Steam-Boat off a Harbour's Mouth", exhibited in 1842 (National Gallery, London).

Watercolour was a less suitable medium for showing the forces of nature at their wildest but such works as "A Tree in a Storm", probably of the 1820s (plate 11), and "Monte Rosa from the Val d'Aosta", the product of a visit to Switzerland in 1836 (plate 22), show how much Turner could accomplish in a small compass. "Monte Rosa", like the Venetian storm scenes of the previous year, is however perhaps more successful in its subtle observation of natural phenomena than in conveying the full power of the elements, which was only fully unleashed in the oil-painting inspired by the same visit,

"Snow-Storm, Avalanche and Inundation – A Scene in the Val d'Aout", exhibited in 1837 and now at Chicago. In the 1840s, though some watercolours such as "Lyons" (plate 25) echo the vortex-like compositions of the oils, there was no attempt to rival their mood.

In the watercolours of Turner's later years there was less difference than before between impressions done for their own sake, sketches done for the engraver and finished works for sale. "Venice from the Lagoon" (plate 18) and "Storm at Venice" (plate 20) were sold to private patrons but there is little distinction in finish between them and other works painted on the same visit which remained in Turner's possession and became part of the Turner Bequest (plates 17 and 19). Watercolours rather than slight pencil drawings began to be used as sketches for oil-paintings, as in the case of some of the Venetian subjects exhibited in the mid 1840s, and in 1842 and 1843 Turner offered, through his dealer Thomas Griffith, to accept commissions for watercolours to be based on existing watercolour sketches made in Switzerland. "Ehrenbreitstein" (plate 28), though not in fact one of these commissioned works, can stand as an example of this group, but again, despite being more heavily worked than say "Freiburg" or "Heidelberg" (plates 27 and 29), it is hardly more finished; similarly, in Turner's oils of the 1840s, the difference between the exhibited and unexhibited works had almost vanished, "Snow-Storm, Steam-Boat off a Harbour's Mouth", exhibited in 1842 (National Gallery, London), being no less daring than the unexhibited "Yacht approaching the Coast" of about the same date (Tate Gallery).

At the same time the distinction in purpose between pencil and water-colour sketches diminished: Turner's pencil drawings became less of a factual record or reminder and his watercolours less of a complete pictorial statement. The pencil drawing underlying a watercolour was often left to play an important part in the composition, as in plates 27, 29 and 31, instead of being covered over, and drawing with pen or brush was used more and more for suggesting detail in more finished works (see plates 25 and 28). In addition the distinction between Turner's watercolour and oil technique often nearly disappeared, the delicate glazes of such an oil-painting as "Norham Castle" (Tate Gallery) being floated over the white ground just like watercolour over paper. Turner's late watercolours, as represented by the last nine plates in this book, are thus both infinitely more varied in their subtle differences and at the same time more unified in style than a parallel group of earlier works such as plates 11 to 14.

Turner's late watercolours are the complete fulfilment of the promise of the Venetian sketches of 1819. After the concentration on colour alone in the works in body-colour of about 1825–35 Turner's new flexibility of technique enabled him to combine colour with a full realisation of light and atmosphere. In some of the late works colour is divorced from appearances, but Turner, never one to be content with the mere recording of nature, was now able, on the basis of a life-time of observation, to create a reality of his own that is entirely convincing, whether comprising mauve buildings and red cows (plate 32), scarlet whales (plate 31) or merely the intangible atmosphere of the sun-baked Italian Campagna (plate 30). Technique and content are one; whereas in some of his late oils Turner expressed his final pessimistic judgment on the weakness of man before the irrational and irresistible forces of nature, the pure and luminous tones of the watercolours expressed his belief in its beneficent qualities.

Turner's last dateable watercolours are from 1845, the year of his last journey abroad; his last dateable pencil sketches are in the Kent sketchbook of the same or the following year. Though some of the vast number of undated watercolours in the Turner Bequest may be later, it is probable that in watercolours, as in oils, the last five years of Turner's life saw the virtual extinction of his creative powers. 1846 was the last year in which the Royal Academy exhibition included recent works by him of any quality. In 1847 he disinterred a work of some thirty years earlier and partly overpainted it; in 1848 there was nothing, in 1849 two early works, one completely repainted. Finally, in 1850, he produced four new paintings, probably painted over earlier colour lay-ins, on the theme of Dido and Aeneas, stereotyped in composition, hot in colour and clumsy in handling. The following year he attended the varnishing days but had no works on view, and on the 19th December 1851 he died.

By the terms of Turner's will the finished paintings he still owned were to go to the British nation, while the proceeds of his estate were to be used for the foundation of a home for poor artists. The will was disputed by his relations and the result, after five years, was that they received his money while the entire accumulation of paintings, watercolours and drawings in his possession at his death went to the nation. The watercolours and drawings, many in the original sketchbooks and numbering nearly 20,000 in all, are now housed in the Department of Prints and Drawings at the British Museum, though selections are on view during the winter months at the Tate Gallery and elsewhere. The watercolours in other collections tend to be the more finished works that Turner was prepared to sell during his lifetime.

In the commentaries on the plates which follow, works in the Turner Bequest are identified by the numbers in A. J. Finburg's published inventory of 1909. This and other publications are referred to in an abbreviated form; full title and place of publication are given in the Bibliography on page 15. Exhibitions, unless otherwise stated, were of Turner's works only and took place in London. In the measurements height precedes width.

I am grateful to the owners of the works reproduced for allowing them to be specially photographed for this book, often at considerable inconvenience. Among the many people who have helped me with advice or in other ways I must single out the staff of the Department of Prints and Drawings at the British Museum and Mr. Evelyn Joll, who has given me the benefit of the vast amount of information about Turner accumulated by Messrs. Thos. Agnew and Sons over the last century. Mr. Adrian Stokes kindly read my text and made a number of suggestions.

Chronology

All exhibitions took place in London unless the contrary is stated.

1775   23rd April. Born in London.

1786   First signed and dated drawing.

1789   Probable date of first sketches from nature. – Began four years study at the Royal Academy Schools. – Studied with Thomas Malton at much the same time.

1790   First exhibit, a watercolour, at the Royal Academy.

1791   First of frequent sketching tours throughout Britain to collect topographical material.

1792   First visit to Wales.

1794   Publication of the first engraving after one of his watercolours. – Probable date of the first of three years during which he spent the winter evenings copying drawings by J. R. Cozens at Dr. Monro's; met Girtin there.

1796   Exhibited his first oil-painting at the Royal Academy.

1797   First visit to the Lake District.

1799   Elected an Associate of the Royal Academy.

1801   First visit to Scotland.

1802   Full member of the Royal Academy. – First visit to France and Switzerland.

1805   First exhibition of his works at his own gallery.

1806   Two oil-paintings at the first exhibition of the British Institution; from then on usually exhibited both here and at the Royal Academy, as well as at his own gallery.

1807   Publication of the first large subscription engraving after one of his oils, and of the first volume of the *Liber Studiorum*. – Elected Professor of Perspective at the Royal Academy.

1810   First recorded visit to Walter Fawkes of Farnley Hall; he made almost yearly visits up to 1824.

1817   First visit to the Low Countries and the Rhine Valley.

1819   Exhibitions of his works at the London homes of two of his chief patrons, Walter Fawkes and Sir John Leicester. – First visit to Italy: Venice, Rome and Naples.

1821   Visited Paris and Normandy.

1822   Groups of watercolours made for engravings exhibited by the publisher W. B. Cooke; also in 1823 and 1824.

1825   Visited the Low Countries and the Rhine.

1826   Visited the Meuse, the Moselle, Brittany and the Loire.

1827   Stayed with John Nash, the architect, on the Isle of Wight.

1828   Second visit to Rome; some of his works on view to the public there.

1829   A group of engraved watercolours exhibited at the Egyptian Hall and in Birmingham. – Visited Paris, Normandy and Brittany. – His period of greatest activity at Petworth probably followed the death of his father in the September of this year.

1832   A group of engraved watercolours exhibited at Moon, Boys and Graves, also in 1833 and 1834.

1834   Illustrations to Byron exhibited at Colnaghi's. Four of his early oil-paintings exhibited at the Society of British Artists. – Visited the Meuse, Moselle and Rhine.

1835   Second visit to Venice almost certainly this year.

1836   Visited France and Switzerland with H.A.J.Munro of Novar. – Ruskin's first letter to Turner.

1837   Represented in the British Institution's *Old Masters* exhibition.

1840   Met Ruskin for the first time. – Third visit to Venice.

1841   Visited Switzerland; again in 1842 and 1844.

1843   Publication of the first volume of Ruskin's *Modern Painters*, largely devoted to Turner.

1845   Represented at the Congress of European Art exhibition in Munich. – Two short visits to the French coast, his last journeys abroad.

1848   One oil-painting hung in the National Gallery to represent the Vernon Bequest of contemporary British painting.

1849   Represented in the British Institution's *Old Masters* exhibition.

1851   19th December. Died at Chelsea. Buried in St. Paul's on 30th December.

Select Bibliography

MONOGRAPHS AND GENERAL WORKS

JOSEPH FARINGTON, Manuscript Diary, 1793–1821, in the Royal Library, Windsor; a selection is published as *The Farington Diary*, edited by James Grieg, 8 vols., London, 1922–8.

JOHN RUSKIN, *Modern Painters*, 5 vols., London, 1843–60; the complete writings of Ruskin are reprinted in *The Works of Ruskin*, *Library Edition*, 59 vols., London, 1903–12 (the last volume is a fully classified index).

JOHN RUSKIN, *Pre-Raphaelitism*, London, 1851.

JOHN BURNET, *Turner and his Works*, with a "Memoir" by Peter Cunningham, London, 1852; 2nd edition, 1859.

ALARIC A. WATTS, "Biographical Sketch", in Leitch Ritchie, *Liber Fluviorum; or River Scenery of France*, London, 1853.

THOMAS MILLER, "Memoirs of Turner and Girtin", in *Turner and Girtin's Picturesque Views Sixty Years Since*, London, 1854.

WALTER THORNBURY, *Life of J. M. W. Turner, R. A.*, 2 vols., London, 1862; 2nd edition in one vol., London, 1877.

RICHARD AND SAMUEL REDGRAVE, *A Century of British Painters*, 2 vols., London, 1866.

C. F. BELL, *The Exhibited Works of J. M. W. Turner, R. A.*, London, 1901.

SIR WALTER ARMSTRONG, *Turner*, London, Manchester, Liverpool and New York, 1902.

CHARLES HOLME (ed.), *The Genius of J. M. W. Turner, R. A.*, London, Paris and New York, 1903.

THEODORE ANDREA COOK, *The Water-Colour Drawings of J. M. W. Turner, R. A., in the National Gallery*, London, Paris, New York and Melbourne, 1904.

E. T. COOK, *Hidden Treasures at the National Gallery*, London, 1905.

W. G. RAWLINSON, *The Engraved Work of J. M. W. Turner, R. A.*, 2 vols., London, 1908 and 1913.

W. G. RAWLINSON AND A. J. FINBERG, *The Water-Colours of J. M. W. Turner*, London, Paris and New York, 1909.

A. J. FINBERG, *Turner's Sketches and Drawings*, London, 1910.

A. J. FINBERG, *Turner's Water-Colours at Farnley Hall*, London, Paris and New York, n. d. [1912].

A. J. FINBERG, *Early English Water-Colour Drawings by the Great Masters*, London, Paris and New York, 1919.

A. J. FINBERG, *The History of Turner's Liber Studiorum with a New Catalogue Raisonné*, London, 1924.

THOMAS ASHBY, *Turner's Visions of Rome*, London and New York, 1925.

A. P. OPPÉ (introd.), *The Water-Colours of Turner, Cox and de Wint*, London and New York, 1925.

WILLIAM T. WHITLEY, *Artists and their Friends in England, 1700–1799*, vol. II, London and Boston, 1928.

WILLIAM T. WHITLEY, *Art in England 1800–1820*, Cambridge, 1928.

A. J. FINBERG, *In Venice with Turner*, London, 1930.

WILLIAM T. WHITLEY, *Art in England 1821–1837*, Cambridge, 1930.

LAURENCE BINYON, *English Watercolours*, London, 1933.

CAMBELL DODGSON (introd.), *6 Aquarelle von J. M. W. Turner*, Vienna, 1937.

A. J. FINBERG, *The Life of J. M. W. Turner, R. A.*, Oxford, 1939; 2nd edition, revised and with a supplement by Hilda F. Finberg, Oxford, 1961.

HANS VOLLMER, "Turner, William", in Thieme-Becker, *Allgemeines Lexicon der Bildenden Kunst*, vol. XXXIII, Leipzig, 1939.

KENNETH CLARK, *Landscape into Art*, London, 1949.

CHARLES CLARE, *J. M. W. Turner, his Life and Work*, London, 1951.

T. S. R. BOASE, *English Art 1800–1870*, Oxford, 1959.

ADRIAN STOKES, "The Art of Turner (1775–1851)", part 3 of *Painting and the Inner World*, London, 1963.

EDWARD CROFT-MURRAY, "Watercolors from The Turner Bequest", in *Exhibition Catalogue, Washington and American tour*, 1963–4.

JOHN ROTHENSTEIN AND MARTIN BUTLIN, *Turner*, London, 1964.

ARTICLES

"The Private Collections of England: Farnley Hall, Otley", in *Athenæum*, 1879, vol. II, pp. 406–8, 439–40, 470–2, 501–3, 600–1, 636–7.

EDWARD DILLON, "Turner's Last Swiss Drawings", in *Art Journal*, 1902, pp. 329–34, 363–6.

A. J. Finberg, "Some So-Called Turners in the Print Room", in *Burlington Magazine*, vol. IX, 1906, pp. 191–5.

A. J. Finberg, "Turner's 'Isle of Wight' Sketch-Book", in *Annual of the Walpole Society*, vol. I, 1911–12, pp. 85–9.

A. J. Finberg, "Some of the Doubtful Drawings in the Turner Bequest at the National Gallery", in *Annual of the Walpole Society*, vol. II, 1912–13, pp. 127–32.

A. J. Finberg, "Some Leaves from Turner's 'South Wales' Sketch-Book", in *Annual of the Walpole Society*, vol. III, 1913–14, pp. 78–97.

Thomas Ashby, "Turner in Rome", in *Burlington Magazine*, vol. XXIV, 1914, pp. 218–24, and vol. XXV, 1914, pp. 98–104.

Thomas Ashby, "Turner at Tivoli", in *Burlington Magazine*, vol. XXV, 1914, pp. 241–7.

C. F. Bell, "Fresh Light on Some Water-Colour Painters of the Old British School: J.M.W. Turner", in *Annual of the Walpole Society*, vol. V, 1915–17, pp. 77–8.

A. J. Finberg, "Further Leaves from Turner's 'South Wales' Sketch-Book", in *Annual of the Walpole Society*, vol. VI, 1917–18, pp. 95–103.

A. J. Finberg, "With Turner at Geneva", in *Apollo*, vol. I, 1925, pp. 38–42.

C. F. Bell and Thomas Girtin, "The Drawings and Sketches of John Robert Cozens", part IX, in *Annual of the Walpole Society*, vol. XXIII, 1934–5, pp. 20–3.

A. J. Finberg, "Turner's Newly Identified Yorkshire Sketch-Book", in *Connoisseur*, vol. XCVI, 1935, pp. 184–7.

Edward Croft-Murray, "An Unpublished Early Watercolour by J.M.W. Turner: 'Cote House, Bristol'", in *Burlington Magazine*, vol. XC, 1948, pp. 106–9.

Kenneth Clark, "Turner at Petworth", in *Ambassador*, no. 8, 1949, pp. 75–90.

Siegfried Freiberg, "Turner zeichnete in Österreich", in *Alte und Neue Kunst*, vol. IV, 1955, pp. 133–9.

Hilda F. Finberg, "With Mr. Turner in 1797", in *Burlington Magazine*, vol. XCIX, 1957, 48–51.

Ann Livermore, "J. M. W. Turner's Unknown Verse-Book", in *Connoisseur Year Book*, 1957, pp. 78–86.

Ann Livermore, "Turner and Music", in *Music and Letters*, vol. XXXVIII, 1957, pp. 170–9.

Margaret Greenshields, "A Turner Discovery", in *Museum's Journal*, vol. LVII, 1957–8, pp. 288–9.

CATALOGUES

John Ruskin, *Catalogue of the Turner Sketches in the National Gallery*, London, 1857.

John Ruskin, *Catalogue of the Sketches and Drawings by J. M. W. Turner, R.A., Exhibited in Marlborough House in the Year 1857–8*, London, 1857.

John Ruskin, *Catalogue of Drawings by the late J. M. W. Turner, Presented to the Fitzwilliam Museum by John Ruskin, Esq.*, London, n. d. [1861].

John Ruskin, *Notes by Mr. Ruskin on his Drawings by the late J. M. W. Turner, R.A.*, London, 1878.

John Ruskin, *Catalogue of the Drawings and Sketches by J. M. W. Turner, R.A., at Present Exhibited in the National Gallery*, Orpington, 1881.

Catalogue of the Farnley Hall Collection of Pictures and Drawings by J. M. W. Turner, R.A., etc., Messrs. Lawrie & Co's Galleries, London, n.d. [late 1902].

A. J. Finberg, *A Complete Inventory of the Drawings of the Turner Bequest, with which are included the twenty-three drawings bequeathed by Mr. Henry Vaughan*, 2 vols., London, 1909.

Catalogue, *Exhibition of Water-Colour Drawings by Joseph Mallord William Turner R. A.*, Agnew's Galleries, London, April–May 1913.

Commemorative Catalogue of the Exhibition of British Art, Royal Academy of Arts, London, January–March, 1934, London, 1935.

Catalogue, *Centenary Loan Exhibition of Water-Colour Drawings by J. M. W. Turner, R.A.*, Thos. Agnew and Sons, Ltd., London, February–March, 1951.

Exhibition Catalogue, *Water Colours by J. M. W. Turner, R. A.*, City of Manchester Art Gallery, December 1952–January 1953.

Exhibition Catalogue, *J. M. W. Turner R. A., 1775–1851*, Whitechapel Art Gallery, London, February–March, 1953.

Exhibition Catalogue, *Turner in America*, John Herron Art Museum, Indianapolis, November–December 1955.

Exhibition Catalogue, *The Romantic Movement*, Tate Gallery and Arts Council Gallery, London, July–September, 1959.

Exhibition Catalogue, *J. M. W. Turner, R. A., 1775–1851*, Leggatt Brothers, London, Autumn 1960.

Exhibition Catalogue, *Joseph Mallord William Turner, Watercolours and Drawings*, Otto Gerson Gallery, New York, November–December 1960.

Exhibition Catalogue, *J.M.W. Turner (1775–1851), Watercolours*, National Gallery of Victoria, Melbourne, September–October 1961.

Plates

1   Christk Church from the Meadows

1799. Watercolour and pen over pencil, 12¹/₂×17³/₄ in. (31.3×45.1 cm.). Oxford, the Ashmolean Museum (on permanent deposit from the Delegates of the Oxford University Press).

COLLECTION: *The Oxford University Press since 1799.*

EXHIBITED: British Art, 1000–1860, *Royal Academy, winter 1934 (714; Souvenir Catalogue 758).*

ENGRAVED: *J. Basire 1799, for the* Oxford Almanac, *1799; J. Skelton 1820–28, for his* Oxonia Antiqua Restaurata.

LITERATURE: *W. G. Rawlinson, "Turner's Drawings at the Royal Academy", in* The Ninteenth Century, *1886, p. 404; Armstrong, 1902, p. 269; C. F. Bell, "The Oxford Almanacs", in* Art Journal, *1904, p. 243; Rawlinson,* Engraved Work, *vol. I, 1908, pp. xx–xxi, 13–15 and vol. II, 1913, p. 188.*

This watercolour was painted for the *Oxford Almanac* of 1799; Turner also did the designs for the issues of every year between 1801 and 1811 with the exception of 1803 and 1810. He was paid ten guineas for each subject. There are two related pencil drawings in the British Museum, one, watermarked 1794, among a group of miscellaneous sketches (Turner Bequest L–Q), the other from a sketchbook also watermarked 1794, but containing drawings made when Turner visited Fonthill in the summer of 1799, together with other sketches made as late as 1801 (Turner Bequest XLVIII–2).

Perhaps on account of its purpose this work was painted in the deliberate, careful technique and cool subdued tonality of the traditional topographical watercolour that Turner had largely abandoned by this time. The views of Fonthill, for instance, which resulted from the visit of 1799, some of which were exhibited at the Royal Academy in 1800 (Brodick Castle, Arran; British Museum, Turner Bequest LXX–P, etc.), are stormier in mood, freer in execution and warmer in tone, lacking the all-pervading grey washes that underlie the Oxford watercolour. A comparison with plate 4, a similar scene of meadows and mellow sunlight painted in 1809, shows the extent of the transformation of Turner's style during these years.

2 Edinburgh from the West, the Water of Leith in the Foreground

1801. Pencil and watercolour, $4^{15}/_{16} \times 7^{5}/_{8}$ in. (12.5×19.4 cm.). London, the British Museum (Turner Bequest LV–1).
LITERATURE: *Finberg*, Turner Bequest, *1909, vol. I, p. 141; Finberg*, Life, *1939, pp. 73–5.*

This is the first page of Turner's "Edinburgh" sketchbook, so labelled by the artist himself and watermarked with the date 1794. Turner set out from London on his first visit to Scotland in the middle of June 1801 and reached Edinburgh on about the 10th July, leaving again on the 18th for the Highlands; he left Scotland on the 5th August. The chief results of this tour were over two hundred pencil sketches and over fifty finished drawings in chalk and pencil on paper prepared with a yellowish-brown wash; there were also the four miraculous wash-drawings in this sketchbook. Turner painted a few finished watercolours, presumably on his return, such as "Edinburgh New Town, castle etc. from the Water of Leith", exhibited at the Royal Academy in 1802 (Lord Joicey).

In this watercolour sketch and its companions in the sketchbook Turner used the restricted colour range of his earlier works in an entirely new way: over a slight pencil outline he built up a complete impression of form and colour by the juxtaposition and superimposition of flat washes in three basic tints. The result is of an almost Chinese delicacy. The Castle Rock, seen above the intervening early morning mists, has a feeling of hovering lightness akin to that, for example, of the distant hills in the oil-painting "Morning amongst the Coniston Fells", exhibited in 1798 (Tate Gallery), while the absence of foreground detail leaves it as the dominant feature in the composition.

3 Scene on the Thames with Rainbow

Circa 1806. Watercolour over pen on paper prepared with a grey wash, 6³/₄×
10³/₈ *in.* (17.2×26.3 *cm.*). *London, the British Museum (Turner Bequest
XCIII–40 a).*
LITERATURE: *Finberg*, Turner Bequest, *1909, vol. I, p. 243; Finberg,* Life, *1939,
p. 137.*

This is a page from the "Hesperides" sketchbook, which was so labelled by Turner
and contains sketches for the oil-painting "The Goddess of Discord choosing the
apple of contention in the garden of the Hesperides", exhibited at the Royal
Academy in 1806, and for a number of other oils exhibited in subsequent years;
the Thames scenes occupy the last ten pages of the book.

The years in which Turner made sketching trips on the Thames are not preci-
sely documented – it was of course within easy reach of London – but Finberg has
narrowed down the likely date of at least the most important of these to 1807.
Turner had, however, already exhibited some oil-paintings of the Thames at his
own gallery in the spring of that year, and the rather classical compositions of
this particular group of Thames watercolours, one of which (XCIII–38a) is particularly Poussinesque in character, suggest that they may date from a year or so
earlier. The handling of this group, a bolder version of the technique of the
Edinburgh sketch on plate 2, is rather flat and schematised, unlike the
fresh and atmospheric watercolours in the "Thames from Reading to Walton"
sketchbook (British Museum, Turner Bequest XCV), which, like the still more revolutionary oil sketches on mahogany veneer in the Tate Gallery, can more certainly be ascribed to the year 1807. Nevertheless this work is significant in showing
Turner's return to a closer study of nature after his predominating interest in
large storm-scenes and subject-pictures during the five preceding years.

The use of tinted paper reflects Turner's interest in different grounds. The
finished "Scottish pencils" of 1801 had been drawn over a yellowish-brown wash
and in the oil sketches on wood of 1807 Turner made use of the colouristic effect
of the mahogany veneer; in another sketchbook of this time, the "Sussex"
sketchbook (British Museum, Turner Bequest XCII), he experimented with green
and deep purple tints. These grounds produced a middle tone from which he could
work both towards the darks and towards the lights, the latter being achieved, in
his watercolours, by the scratching or washing out of the ground to reveal the white
paper below; here scratching-out is used in the rainbow and in the foreground.

4 Bolton Abbey, Wharfedale

1809. Signed "J. M. W. Turner RA PP 1809" lower right. Watercolour with some glue or oil medium, 10¹⁵/₁₆×15¹/₂ in. (27.8×39.4 cm.). London, the British Museum (1910-2-12-282).

COLLECTIONS: *? Walter Fawkes; ? J. E. Taylor 1877; George Salting, bought 1899 and bequeathed to the British Museum 1910.*

EXHIBITED: *? Walter Fawkes collection, 45 Grosvenor Place, April–June 1819 (23); ? Old Master Drawings, Grosvenor Galleries, Winter 1877–8 (268, lent by J. E. Taylor); Guildhall, 1899 (132); Collection of the Late Mr. George Salting, Agnew, January 1910 (223); exhibition of the Salting Bequest, British Museum, 1910.*

ENGRAVED: *E. Finden 1826, for The Literary Souvenir, 1826, pl. 9.*

LITERATURE: *Armstrong, 1902, p. 243, repr. p. 63; Rawlinson, Engraved Work, vol. II, 1913, pp. 196, 220; Finberg, Life, 1939, pp. 480 (no. 232), 504 (no. 519).*

This late afternoon view of Bolton Abbey from the north is a companion work to the undated view of the abbey from the south which is still at Farnley Hall. It was almost certainly one of the two watercolours of the abbey shown by Walter Fawkes as part of his collection at his London house in 1819; the first big sale of works from this collection took place at Christie's in 1890, but this work was not included in this or any subsequent sale and must have been sold or given away

earlier. The letters "RA" and "PP" following the signature stand for Royal Academician and Professor of Perspective, an office of the Academy to which Turner was elected in 1807.

Turner's association with Walter Fawkes of Farnley Hall was, with the exception of that with Lord Egremont at Petworth (see plates 14 and 15), the most fruitful of his career, seven oils and about two hundred watercolours having entered Walter Fawkes' collection by his death in 1825. Their acquaintance seems to have begun in 1802 when Turner was commissioned to work up some of his Swiss sketches; his first recorded visit to Farnley occurred in 1810. Between 1815 and 1824 he seems to have gone there at least once a year and he continued to receive a Christmas hamper of game and goose-pie from the Fawkes family up to his own death in 1851. The two most important groups of watercolours painted for Walter Fawkes are the Yorkshire scenes in the neighbourhood of Farnley Hall and those resulting from Turner's Rhine journey of 1817 (see plates 5 and 6). This watercolour of 1809 would be one of the earliest of the first group, on which Turner seems to have worked until about 1818.

An anonymous series of articles on the Farnley Hall collection in the *Athenæum* of 1879 describes the companion "Bolton Abbey from the South" but concludes with a passage equally applicable to this example (vol. II, p. 471): "A peculiarly delicious study in Turner's mode of employing a general greenish olive tint, and a wonderful rendering of pale golden light." It shows the application of the new degree of naturalism found in the Thames sketches of two or three years earlier in the context of the finished watercolour, but the composition is more artificial and carefully arranged. The foreground is raised and trees frame the scene, and particularly the abbey itself; the winding river leads the eye into the distance, where one sees the rising smoke pointed out by Ruskin as one of Turner's favourite motives.

Even in this disciplined vision of the English countryside, however, Turner's technique shows a marked advance on that of his early topographical watercolours such as plate 1. The tonality is lighter and lacks the colouristically neutral monochrome washes that determined the shadows of the early works. The handling includes scratching-out in the foreground and river and drawing with the handle of the brush in the wet gummy medium used for the browns of the foliage; this use of an oil or gummy medium was developed from the small oil sketches on paper painted at Knockholt in 1806 (British Museum, Turner Bequest XCV(a)).

5 Mainz and Kastell

1817. *Watercolour with touches of body-colour*, $8^3/_{16} \times 14^3/_8$ in. (20.8 × 36.5 cm.). *Chobham, Capt. The Hon. Nicholas Beaumont.*

COLLECTIONS: *Walter Fawkes 1817; Frederick Hawksworth Fawkes, sold 1912 to Agnew, from whom bought by W. H. Jones c. 1924; sale of the late Mrs. Walter Jones, Christie's 3 July 1942 (51), bought by Gooden and Fox; 2nd Viscount Allendale.*

EXHIBITED: Old Masters, *Royal Academy, winter 1889 (23); Lawrie Galleries, 1902 (21); Agnew's Exchange Street Galleries, Manchester, 1912 (3); Agnew, 1913 (49);* Selected Water Colour Drawings, *Agnew, 1919 (17);* Annual Exhibition of Water Colour Drawings, *Agnew, 1924 (21);* British Art, 1000–1860, *Royal Academy, winter 1934 (904;* Souvenir Catalogue *765); Agnew, 1951 (57).*

LITERATURE: *Ruskin,* Pre-Raphaelitism, *1851 (Library Edition, vol. XII, 1904, pp. 376–8); Thornbury, 1862, vol. II, pp. 86–7, 394 (1877 edition, pp. 238, 591); Athenæum, 1879, vol. II, pp. 406, 637; Armstrong, 1902, p. 265 (the first work listed as "Mainz"); Finberg,* Farnley Hall, *1912, pp. 8–10, 23, repr. in colour pl. 18; Finberg,* Life, *1939, pp. 249–50.*

This is one of fifty-one watercolours of views on the Rhine painted by Turner in 1817 and sold on his return to Walter Fawkes for £500. Turner left London on the 10th August and, after visiting Brussels and the battlefield of Waterloo, reached Cologne on the 18th August; he went up the Rhine as far as Mainz where he stayed on the 25th and 26th, and was back at Cologne for the 29th and 30th. He returned to England via Rotterdam and probably Hull, visited Raby Castle in connection with the oil painting now at Baltimore, and arrived at Farnley Hall on the 15th November with the fifty-one completed drawings in his pocket; his speed of execution was, perhaps pardonably, exaggerated by Thornbury.

Turner used two small sketchbooks and one somewhat larger one on his tour of the Rhine. This watercolour seems to have been based on a slight drawing filling no more than a third of a page of one of the former (British Museum, Turner Bequest CLX–70), supplemented by Turner's remarkable visual memory.

This open view of the Rhine, like other examples in the series, has a luminosity that foreshadows the watercolours made on Lake Como and at Venice two years later (see plate 9). The heavy black cloud hovers above the transparent foreground and between them Turner used his favourite device, developed in his early sea-pieces, of a brightly lit strip of distant water which both draws the eye into depth and helps to prevent this feeling of depth from disrupting the unified design of the surface. Turner's skill at suggesting realistic appearances by unrealistic means is typified by the fact that the sky is more solidly painted than the water.

This work is also a fine example of the variety of touch used by Turner. The louring rain-cloud in the centre was painted while the paper was wet, the pink washes and touches of buff body-colour, drawn with the point of the brush, being added when the paper had dried. Conversely, the distant town shows the effect of using very dilute washes on dry paper. In the foreground the texture of the boats and surrounding water has been indicated by dragging relatively dry washes over the surface of the paper, while a line drawn by a wet brush through these washes has described a ripple on the smooth water; a similar use of washing-out produced the distant white sail and its reflection on the left. Another textural effect is that of the artist's finger-prints in the water above the rowing boat.

6 From Rheinfels,
looking over St. Goar to Katz

COLLECTIONS: *Walter Fawkes 1817; Frederick Hawksworth Fawkes, from whom bought by Agnew 1912; T. A. Tatton, sold at Christie's 14 December 1928 (35), bought by Agnew; Lord Horder, sold anonymously at Sotheby's 10 December 1958 (102, repr.), bought by Agnew, from whom bought by George Goyder 1959.*

EXHIBITED: Old Masters, *Royal Academy, winter 1889 (49); Lawrie Galleries, 1902 (19); Agnew's Exchange Street Galleries, Manchester, 1912 (75); Agnew, 1913 (48); Agnew, 1951 (60);* Annual Water-Colour Exhibition, *Agnew, 1959 (47).*

LITERATURE: *Ruskin*, Pre-Raphaelitism, *1851 (Library Edition, vol. XII, 1904, pp. 376–8); Thornbury, 1862, vol. II, 86–7, 395 (1877 edition, pp. 238, 591); Athenæum, 1879, vol. II, pp. 406, 637; Armstrong, 1902, p. 272; Finberg, Farnley Hall, 1912, pp. 8–10, 24, repr. in colour pl. 29; Finberg*, Life, *1939, pp. 249–50.*

This is another example of the fifty-one Rhine watercolours made in 1817 and sold to Walter Fawkes. It is based on drawings in Turner's larger "Rhine" sketchbook, particularly page 42 (British Museum, Turner Bequest CLXI–42; see also 22a and 23), made on his return journey down the Rhine. He was at St. Goar on the 27th August, having already stayed there on his outward journey on the 23rd and 24th.

Ruskin says of the group, "Every one of these sketches is the almost instantaneous record of an *effect* of colour or atmosphere, taken strictly from nature, the drawing and the details of every subject being comparatively subordinate, and the colour nearly as principal as the light and shade had been before [in Turner's earlier topographical watercolours (see plates 1 and 4)]. And naturally, as the colour becomes the leading object, those times of day are chosen in which it is most lovely; ... we now find his attention directed constantly to the evening: and, for the first time, we have those rosy lights upon the hills, those gorgeous falls of sun through flaming heavens, those solemn twilights, with the blue moon rising as the western sky grows dim, which have ever since been the themes of his mightiest thoughts. I have no doubt, that the *immediate* reason of this change was the impression made upon him by the colours of the continental skies." This last sentence was partly coloured by Ruskin's belief that the Rhine watercolours were painted on the same journey as Turner's first eye-opening visit to Italy in 1819 (see plate 9).

1817. Watercolour with touches of body-colour on grey paper, 7⁵/₈×12¹/₄ *in. (19.4×31.1 cm.). Henley-on-Thames, Mr. George Goyder.*

30

7 Sky Study

Circa 1818. Watercolour, 4⁷/₈×9⁵/₈ in. (12.4×24.5 cm.). *London, the British Museum (Turner Bequest* CLVIII–25*).*

LITERATURE: *Finberg*, Turner Bequest, *1909, vol. I, p. 452; Laurence Binyon,* English Water-Colours, *London, 1933, pp. 131–2 (2nd edition, 1944, pp. 115–6).*

This sketch is from the "Skies" sketchbook, so labelled by Turner and water-marked 1814; it contains seventy-nine sketches of skies, together with some pencil drawings of London and Windsor. Two of the drawings apparently show the 4th June celebrations at Eton, which Turner is recorded as having seen with the Fawkes family in 1818.

An enormous range of different sky effects is shown in the sketchbook, including twilight and night scenes. Many of these effects rule out the possibility of Turner having depicted them on the spot, though some of the day-time studies such as this one, which come at the beginning of the book, may have been done out of doors like the comparable works of Constable.

This book of sketches is a good example of Turner's varied use of watercolour to produce different effects. In this example the greyish-blues and pinks of the clouds were mixed very wet, in contrast to the blue washes of more usual consistency used for the sky. On another page the grey washes have been worked on the paper to produce streaks and wisps of cloud. Other sketches are richer in colour, sometimes with strong oranges, similarly worked with a wet brush to show crescent moons or other forms.

CLVIII — 25

8 A First Rate Taking in Stores

*1818. Signed "J. M. W. Turner 1818" lower right. Watercolour and pencil,
11¹/₄×15⁵/₈ in. (28.6×39.7 cm.). Bedford, the Cecil Higgins Art Gallery. (Reproduced by courtesy of the Trustees of the Cecil Higgins Art Gallery.)*
COLLECTIONS: *Walter Fawkes 1818; Walter Ramsden Fawkes, sold Christie's 2
July 1937 (44, repr.), bought by Tooth's; Sir David Eccles; Agnew, from whom
bought by the Cecil Higgins Museum 1953.*
EXHIBITED: *Walter Fawkes collection, 45 Grosvenor Place, April–June 1819 (20),
and Music Hall, Leeds, 1839 (14); Lawrie Galleries, 1902 (29);* Exhibition of
Old Masters in aid of the National Art-Collections Fund, *Grafton Galleries,
October–December 1911 (205); Agnew, 1951 (46); Huntington Library, San
Marino, 1952;* Primitives to Picasso, *Royal Academy, January–March 1962
(382).*
LITERATURE: *Ruskin,* Pre-Raphaelitism, *1851 (Library Edition, vol. XII, 1904,
p. 386, repr. pl. 21); Thornbury, 1862, vol. II, pp. 88, 393 (1877 edition, pp.
239, 589); Athenæum, 1879, vol. II, p. 472; Ruskin,* The Ruskin Cabinet at
Whitelands College. Notes on Sixty Pictures, *1883, no. 32 (Library Edition, vol.
XXX, 1907, p. 352); Armstrong, 1902, pp. 87–8, 253; Alexander J. Finberg,
"The Historical Collection of British Water-Colours at the Grafton Galleries,
Part II", in* Connoisseur, *vol. XXXII, 1912, p. 106, repr.; Finberg,* Farnley
Hall, *1912, pp. 10–11, 25, repr. in colour pl. 8; Finberg,* Life, *1939, pp. 254,
480 (no. 229), 502 (no. 487); Catalogue,* Water-Colours and Drawings in the
Cecil Higgins Collection, *Bedford, 1959, p. 29 (no. P. 99), repr. pl. 8.*

34

This watercolour was painted for Walter Fawkes in November 1818 during one
of Turner's visits to Farnley Hall. The circumstances became a legend in the
Fawkes family. The fullest version is that given in a typescript account by Mrs.
Edith Mary Fawkes, daughter-in-law of Walter Fawkes' third son the Rev. Ayscough Fawkes, now in the library of the National Gallery, London:

"There is one thing quite certain as to the Turner traditions at Farnley for I
have heard it repeatedly stated by all the generation who were children when
Turner was so much at Farnley, and that is, that, with one deeply interesting
exception, no one ever saw him paint when he was there. The exception was this
– one morning at breakfast Walter Fawkes said to him, 'I want you to make me a
drawing of the ordinary dimensions that will give some idea of the size of a man
of war.' The idea hit Turner's fancy, for with a chuckle he said to Walter
Fawkes' eldest son [Francis Hawksworth Fawkes], then a boy of about 15, 'Come
along Hawkey and we will see what we can do for Papa', and the boy sat by his
side the whole morning and witnessed the evolution of 'The First Rate Taking
in Stores'. His description of the way Turner went to work was very extra-
ordinary; he began by pouring wet paint onto the paper till it was saturated, he
tore, he scratched, he scrubbed at it in a kind of frenzy and the whole thing was
chaos – but gradually and as if by magic the lovely ship, with all its exquisite
minutia, came into being and by luncheon time the drawing was taken down in
triumph. I have heard my Uncle give these particulars dozens of times..."

This account, which tallies with Thornbury's earlier version with its graphic
description of how Turner "tore up the sea with his eagle-claw of a thumb-
nail...", illustrates the surprising freedom and virtuosity of Turner's mature
watercolour technique even in his most finished works, a technique in marked
contrast to that of his early topographical drawings such as plate 1. A particular
point to note is the use of a wet brush to remove colour, not only in the sea, but
in the tiny figures and detailed forms on the ship in the foreground; the texture
of the rope is suggested by scratching away the wet paint.

Turner's skilful use of light in the composition is equally unobtrusive. As in
many of his works the eye is drawn towards a distant illuminated area, in this
case a ship, placed directly above the darkest part of the picture; this area is also
slightly emphasised by the delicate clouds above, which themselves contrast with
the rough sea below. The local colour of the flags and uniformed figures are
echoed in broader, paler tones in the sky and on the ships and are subdued to the
general tone of the painting.

9 San Georgio from the Dogana, Venice: Sunrise

1819. Watercolour, 8¹³/₁₆×11⁵/₁₆ in. (22.4×28.7 cm.). London, the British Museum (Turner Bequest CLXXXI–4).
EXHIBITED: Turner Watercolors, *Washington, Houston, San Francisco, Cleveland, Kansas City and Brooklyn, 1963–4 (16, repr. in colour on cover).*
LITERATURE: *Finberg*, Turner Bequest, *1909, vol. I, p. 535; Finberg*, Venice, *1930, pp. 22, 167, repr. in colour as frontispiece.*

This watercolour, painted in Venice in 1819, comes from Turner's "Como" sketchbook (watermarked 1816); besides the Venetian watercolours the book contains two of Lake Como, two stormy coast scenes probably made on the Adriatic coast as Turner proceeded to Rome, and four lay-ins of three basic colours representing the foreground, distance and sky, of a kind that may have been the starting point for some of the other sketches.

This was Turner's first visit to Italy. He left London early in August 1819, travelling by way of Paris, Lyons and the Mont Cenis Pass to Turin; he then visited the North Italian Lakes before arriving at Venice, where he seems to have stayed for about a month, leaving for Rome probably early in October.

That summer Turner had already begun a finished watercolour of Venice for an engraving, based on a drawing by James Hakewill, and the practical results of his visit were slight, only three finished watercolours of 1820 and 1821; he did not exhibit any oil-paintings of Venice until 1833. Even while at Venice he only made four sketches in colour, preferring to spend his time getting to know the city through small pencil drawings, about eighty in number.

But this watercolour shows the revolutionary effect of the impact of Italy upon Turner's feeling for light and colour, and in particular that of Venice; in comparison, the watercolours of Lake Como and those made a month or two later in Rome (see plate 10) and Naples are much closer to the Rhine drawings of 1817. Here the white of the paper not only lightens the tonality of the superimposed colours, as in many of Turner's earlier watercolours (and as did the white grounds of his oils after about 1810), but it is left to tell in its own right through the most delicate of translucent washes. This manner was not achieved in Turner's oils, nor even in many of his watercolours, until the 1840s. The result is a perfect expression of the freshness of early morning, Turner's summary modelling in flat washes being ideally suited to the *contre-jour* effect.

CLXXXI — 44

10 The Nymphæum of Alexander Severus

After his stay in Venice (see plate 9) Turner went on to Rome, where he probably arrived fairly early in October 1819. He visited Naples and Vesuvius late in that month, returning to Rome by the 15th November. He left for England before the 20th December, and, travelling via Florence, Turin and the Mont Cenis Pass, arrived in London on the 1st February 1820.

As in Venice Turner devoted much of his time in Rome and Naples to making small pencil sketches, but he also filled a number of large sketchbooks with over two hundred and fifty drawings, about forty of them coloured. This activity resulted directly in very few finished works: four watercolours of Rome and two of Naples were painted for Walter Fawkes and two of Vesuvius for other patrons, and oil-paintings of "Rome from the Vatican" and "Forum Romanum" were exhibited at the Royal Academy in 1820 and 1826; "The Bay of Baiae", exhibited in 1823, did however set the pattern for a whole series of Italian landscapes exhibited in the 1820s and 1830s.

This watercolour comes from the sketchbook, watermarked 1816, labelled by Turner as "14 Rome: C. Studies", the "C" probably standing for "Chiaroscuro", most of the drawings being chiaroscuro studies on tinted paper. Ruskin suggests that this work and its companion, the so-called "Claudian Aqueduct" (CLXXXIX–36), are among the rare examples of sketches coloured by Turner on the spot, but against this there is the contemparary account sent from Naples by the son of Sir John Soane the architect, of how, "At Rome a sucking blade of the brush made the request of going out with pig Turner to colour – he grunted for answer that it would take up too much of his time to colour in the open air – he could make 15 or 16 pencil sketches to one coloured." That Turner coloured these sketches when back at his lodgings is supported by Ashby's discovery that the aqueduct which appears in both works is in fact a misinterpretation of the galleries of the Aurelian Wall. In other respects the watercolours are topographically accurate.

In its use of grey prepared paper and its rather sombre colouring this watercolour is closer to the Rhine drawings of 1817 than to the etherial Venetian sketches of earlier in the same year. This however suits the subject and in other watercolours, particularly those of the Roman Campagna and the Bay of Naples, Turner's palette is lighter, though never quite achieving the freshness of the Venetian works. The composition, with the solid mass of the ruined Nymphæum at the left-hand side and the strong horizontal emphasis of the flat plain and the supposed "acqueduct", reflects the discipline that Turner had acquired from his study of Poussin.

1819. Body-colour and watercolour over pencil on paper prepared with a grey wash, $9^1/_{16} \times 14^1/_2$ *in. (23×36.8 cm.). London, the British Museum (Turner Bequest CLXXXIX–35).*

EXHIBITED: W. Blake and J. M. W. Turner, *Bibliothèque Nationale, Paris, January–February, 1937, and Albertina, Vienna, March–April, 1937 (94).*
LITERATURE: *Ruskin,* Sketches and Drawings exhibited in Marlborough House, *1857, no. 225 (Library Edition, vol. XIII, 1904, p. 298); Finberg,* Turner Bequest, *1909, vol. I, p. 563; Ashby, 1925, p. 25 and at pl. 11, repr. in colour; Finberg,* Venice, *1930, p. 67; Finberg,* Life, *1939, pp. 261–2.*

11 A Tree in a Storm

Circa 1820–30. Watercolour with some glue or oil medium, $9^1/_2 \times 11^7/_8$ *in.* (24.2×30.2 cm.). *London, the British Museum (Turner Bequest CCCLXV–27b).*
EXHIBITED : The Romantic Movement, *Tate Gallery, 1959 (455);* J.M.W. Turner Watercolours, *Tokyo and Osaka, 1963 (6b, repr.), and Hong Kong, 1964 (6b).*
LITERATURE : *Finberg,* Turner Bequest, *1909, vol. II, p. 1213.*

Above this watercolour and on the same sheet of paper is a study in grey and blue washes of the sea with stormy clouds and a sailing boat (Turner Bequest CCCLXV–27a); the complete sheet of paper measures $18^7/_8 \times 11^7/_8$ in. (43×30.2 cm.). Turner seems to have begun the watercolour here reproduced with a similarly restricted range of greys and blues, establishing the basic forces of the stormy scene but not the actual forms of the tree in a landscape, which were introduced when he added the greenish-browns, blacks and pinks.

The drama of the scene is expressed in Turner's frenzied handling. The greenish-browns, which seem to include some glue or oil medium, have been worked with his fingers, as is shown by the finger-prints in the lower centre. The dramatic effect of the wind-swept tree is increased by its being silhouetted against the bare white of the paper. Consciously or unconsciously, however, Turner was at pains to preserve the equilibrium of his composition: the diagonal of the tree offsets that of the main stresses of the storm clouds and the design is given a firm basis by the emphatic horizontal of the ground.

The date of this type of sketch is impossible to determine. Though grouped by Finberg with miscellaneous drawings of "after about 1830", the relatively subdued and naturalistic colour suggests a tentative dating in the 1820s.

12 Rouen looking up River

Circa 1825–9. Body-colour and pen on blue paper, irregular, approx. $5^1/_2 \times 7^1/_2$
in. (14×19.1 cm.). *London, the British Museum (Turner Bequest CCLIX–107).*
ENGRAVED: *R. Brandard 1834, for Leitch Ritchie,* Turner's Annual Tour-
Wanderings by the Seine, *1834, pl. 18; Himely (aquatint), n.d.*
LITERATURE: *Rawlinson,* Engraved Work, *vol. I, 1908, pp. lv–lvii, and vol. II,
1913, pp. 200, 213–4, 268, 403, 409; Finberg,* Turner Bequest, *1909, vol. II,
p. 795; Finberg,* Life, *1939, pp. 341–2, 399; Clare, 1951, p. 86, repr. p. 84.*

This is one of over two hundred and fifty drawings in body-colour on blue paper
in the British Museum relating to *The Rivers of France* engravings, which appeared in the three volumes of *Turner's Annual Tour*, published in 1833, 1834
and 1835, the first being devoted to the Loire, the other two to the Seine;
seventeen further drawings connected with the Loire subjects belonged to John
Ruskin and were given by him to the Ashmolean Museum, Oxford. The scheme
was presumably intended as a complement to the various collections of engravings of English views which had occupied Turner more or less continuously from
1811, when he began working on *Picturesque Views of the Southern Coast of England*, and which had included *The Rivers of England* of 1823–7.

Although Turner visited Rouen in 1829 on a tour of the Seine and Normandy,
making sketches for an abortive publication to be called *La Manche, or the
English Channel*, some of which were used in *The Rivers of France*, this work
must have been based on the sketches in the "Rouen" sketchbook of 1821, made
before the destruction of the old spire of the central tower the following year
(British Museum, Turner Bequest CCLVIII; see especially page 22a). It was probably painted before the 1829 visit, by which time the new spire had been under
construction for two years.

The detailed treatment of this sketch made for the engraver is very different
from the broad handling of some of the related but unengraved sketches of the
same period, which are much closer to the works in the same medium done at
Petworth (see plates 14 and 15). It may also be compared with the view of
Whitby reproduced as plate 13, a topographical watercolour of much the same
date on white paper in which the emphasis is on atmosphere rather than colour;
this division of interest was not resolved until the later 1830s.

13 Whitby, Yorkshire

Circa 1825–30. Watercolour, 6^1/$_4$×9^3/$_4$ in. (15.9×24.8 cm.), Henley-on-Thames, Mr. George Goyder.
COLLECTIONS: *J. E. Fordham by 1862; F. N. Fordham; B. G. Fordham, sold at Sotheby's 6 June 1951 (13), bought by Apsley Cherry-Garrard; Mrs. Gordon Mathias, sold at Sotheby's 19 April 1961 (36, repr.), bought by Agnew, from whom bought by George Goyder 1961.*
EXHIBITED: Annual Exhibition of Water-Colours and Drawings, *Agnew, 1964 (53, in first edition only).*
ENGRAVED: *J. Cousen 1844, for* Dr. Broadley's Poems *(unpublished); first published in* Art and Song, *1867.*
LITERATURE: *Thornbury, 1862, vol. II, p. 398 (1877 edition, p. 595); Armstrong, 1902, p. 285; Rawlinson, Engraved Work, vol. II, 1913, p. 325.*

This watercolour is close in size and general style, though more delicate in tone and handling and with less incident, to the view of "Whitby from the South" engraved in 1826 for Part I of *The Ports of England* and now in the British Museum (Turner Bequest CCVIII–I); it probably dates from about the same time or a few years later, certainly not from as late as 1844 when it was itself engraved.

Turner had passed Whitby in 1822 on his journey by sea to Edinburgh to make sketches of George IV's visit there, and his "Scotland. King's Visit" sketchbook (British Museum, Turner Bequest CC) contains a series of small studies of the East coast. But Turner probably also had recourse to sketches made in 1801; one of his sketchbooks made on his return from Scotland in that year contains a wash-drawing of the same view (British Museum, Turner Bequest LIV–83a and 84).

This is a particularly sensitive example of Turner's later topographical style. The atmospheric depiction of the little port is most delicately achieved and the composition is carefully designed to draw one's attention to the town sheltering beneath the ruins of its guardian abbey. The genre incidents in the foreground are typical of Turner's more playful mood in the 1820s but avoid the obtrusive effect of such detail in some of his more finished works.

14 Petworth Lake, Sunset

Circa 1830. Body-colour on blue paper, irregular, approx. $5^3/8 \times 7^3/8$ *in. (13.7 ×*
18.7cm.). London, the British Museum (Turner Bequest CCXLIV–12).
EXHIBITED: *National Museum of Wales, Cardiff, winter 1914–15 (104 or 105,*
as "Lake in Petworth Park, Sunset", or 10, 107 or 108, as "At Petworth").
LITERATURE: *Finberg*, Turner Bequest, *1909, vol. II, p. 774, as "At Petworth";*
Finberg, Life, *1939, p. 325; Clark in* Ambassador, *No. 8, 1949, pp. 75–90.*

The atmosphere at Petworth, the home of the 3rd Earl of Egremont, seems to
have been particularly congenial to Turner's art. Lord Egremont's first purchase
of an oil-painting by Turner was in 1802 and he bought a number of other work
of the same decade, including the commissioned view of "Petworth: Dewy
Morning", exhibited at the Royal Academy in 1810. But the most important
period in their relationship was between the death of Turner's father in 1829
and that of Lord Egremont himself in 1837, during which time Turner was a
frequent and specially-favoured visitor with his own studio; from these years date
the landscapes painted for the dining-room at Petworth and the related sketches
and a number of other oils, including the "Interior at Petworth", now in the
Tate Gallery.

This work, like the next, is one of the hundred or so sketches in body-colour
on blue paper painted at Petworth in the early 1830s. Their technique, which is
close to that of some of the unengraved works in *The Rivers of France* series of
circa 1825–35, is heavier and more opaque than the Venetian works on coloured
paper of 1835: compare for instance the bold use of reds, blues and yellows in the
sky of this example with the more subtle reds, their tones moderated by the
brown of the paper underneath, of plates 17 and 18. In the Petworth drawings
the blue paper functions as a middle tone, like the grey wash ground of the
Thames sketch on plate 3, though here the lights cannot be obtained by revealing
the white paper underneath and white body-colour is used for clouds and reflections in the water; in the Venetian works the paper, a more assimilable brown
(or, in some cases, grey), is far more closely integrated into the general colouring.

15 A Bedroom at Petworth

Circa 1830. Body-colour on blue paper, irregular, approx. $5^5/8 \times 7^1/2$ in. $(14.3 \times 19.1$ cm.$)$. *London, the British Museum (Turner Bequest CCXLIV–69).*
LITERATURE: *Finberg,* Turner Bequest, *1909, vol. II, p. 745; Finberg,* Life, *1939, p. 325; Clark in* Ambassador, *No. 8, 1949, pp. 75–90.*

This is one of a number of interior scenes from the same group of sketches made at Petworth in about 1830 as plate 14 and reflects, though less so than some of the other examples, a renewed interest in figure-subjects which was in part associated with Turner's renewed contact with Lord Egremont. Though Turner had already painted a number of such pictures in the 1820s, including "Jessica", painted at Rome in 1828 and bought by Lord Egremont instead of the landscape "Palestrina" intended for him, his oils of figures in interiors seem all to have been painted at Petworth, beginning with two small panels exhibited in 1831. These figure-subjects, though including such masterpieces as "Music at Petworth" and "The Letter", show weaknesses in the depiction of the human figure, perhaps psychological in origin, which are avoided in the delightfully impressionistic sketches in body-colour. This series of sketches is unparallelled in Turner's work, though at Venice in 1835 he painted a few interiors of his bedroom and, with special effects of lighting which give the theme a more dramatic twist akin to his night scenes with rockets, of theatres and wine-shops.

Though some of the other drawings employ pen as well as body-colour, this example is a masterpiece of suggestion by areas of flat colour alone. Typical of Turner's virtuosity is his use of sponging to differentiate the canopy of the bed from its curtains.

16　The Burning of the Houses of Parliament

1834. Watercolour, $9^3/_{16} \times 12^3/_4$ in. (23.4×32.4 cm.). *London, the British Museum (Turner Bequest CCLXXXIII–6).*

LITERATURE: *Finberg*, Turner Bequest, *1909, vol. II, p. 909; Finberg*, Life, *1939, p. 350.*

This is one of nine watercolour sketches made on the night of the 16th October 1834, when the old Houses of Parliament were destroyed by fire; the Turner Bequest also contains a more finished watercolour made after the event (CCCLXIV–373). The following year Turner exhibited two oils of the scene, the first at the British Institution, the second at the Royal Academy; they are now at Philadelphia and Cleveland respectively. The incident seems to have made a great impression on him: although he had already shown scenes of fire, for instance his watercolours of Vesuvius made both before, on the basis of another's sketches, and during his first visit to Italy, the next few years saw the creation of a number of other pictures of similar subjects, such as "Fire at Sea" (National Gallery, London), "Keelmen heaving in Coals by Night" (exhibited at the Royal Academy in 1835 and now at Washington) and a group of Venetian works (see plate 17).

The sketchbook containing this work is still intact and is a fascinating record of Turner's infrequent use of watercolour for recording his impressions on the spot; no doubt the particular circumstances ruled out any other medium. The nine sketches were painted on one side of the paper only with such haste that they blotted the opposite pages; the remaining twenty-three pages were left blank, the book being reserved for the one subject alone.

17 S. Maria della Salute, Venice: Night Scene with Rockets

Probably 1835. Body-colour and chalks on brown paper, irregular, approx. 9¹/₂×12¹/₄ in. (24.1×31.1 cm.). London, the British Museum (Turner Bequest CCCXVIII–29).

EXHIBITED: Twee Eeuwen Engelsche Kunst, *Stedelijk Museum, Amsterdam, 1936 (242); The Romantic Movement, Tate Gallery, 1959 (452); J.M.W. Turner Watercolours, Tokyo and Osaka, 1963 (24, repr.), and Hong Kong, 1964 (24).*

LITERATURE: *Finberg*, Turner Bequest, *1909, vol. II, p. 1028; Finberg*, Venice, *1930, pp. 93, 176; Finberg*, Life, *1939, pp. 355–6.*

This is one of a group of night scenes with rockets, some, if not all, seen from the top floor of the Hotel Europa, painted in body-colour on brown paper during a visit to Venice which, though not documented, almost certainly took place in 1835: the dramatic effects of light seem to reflect the excitement reawakened in Turner by the burning of Parliament the previous year (see plate 16) and the sketches, though done for their own sake, served as studies for the oil-painting "Juliet and her Nurse" exhibited at the Royal Academy in 1836 (New York, Mrs. Flora Whitney Miller). Besides the sketches at the British Museum there is a more finished painting in body-colour at Edinburgh, also on brown paper and similar in its effects of light, of a "Storm in the Piazza".

In these works Turner used body-colour on tinted paper with even greater virtuosity than in *The Rivers of France* and Petworth drawings (see plates 12, 14 and 15). Although such forms as the gondola are modelled in solid flat washes, the facade of the Salute is suggested by a much more open technique in which the brown ground is left bare between blue and white brush-strokes and heavily dragged washes of white. The red glow below the church blurs the distinction between the steps and the water while the Dogana practically melts away into the deep blue sky, bringing about the blending of material and immaterial elements that Turner carried still further in many of his later works.

18 Venice from the Lagoon

Probably 1835. Watercolour with body-colour, pen, chalk and pencil, 8³/₄×11⁵/₈ in. (22.2×29.5 cm.). Cambridge, the Fitzwilliam Museum (589). (Reproduced by permission of the Syndics of the Fitzwilliam Museum.)
COLLECTIONS: *John Ruskin, presented to the Fitzwilliam Museum 1861.*
LITERATURE: *Ruskin*, Drawings presented to the Fitzwilliam Museum, *1861, no. 23 (Library Edition, vol. XIII, 1904, p. 558); Armstrong, 1902, p. 282; Finberg*, Venice, *1930, 112–3, 160, repr. in colour pl. 21; Finberg*, Life, *1939, p. 355.*

This work is similar in style and technique to the body-colours on brown paper at the British Museum such as plate 17, and must date from the same visit, though in contrast to the dramatic night scene with rockets the mood here is calm and serene.

Ruskin described it as a "First sketch, showing his method of using pencil with colour"; in addition, Turner used pen, black chalk and body-colour, showing his almost extravagently varied richness of technique at this time. The extremes of colour, strong blue washes in the sky, patches of red and white body-colour on the figures and buildings, are contained in a unified whole by the all-pervading tone of the paper, which also has a more specifically colouristic function, enriching the red facade of the building on the right and helping to create the authentic rose-pink of the Doge's Palace.

19 Venice from Fusina (?)

Probably 1835. Watercolour, $9^1/_2 \times 11^7/_8$ *in.* (24.1×30.2 cm.). *London, the British Museum (Turner Bequest CCCXVI–25).*
LITERATURE: *Ruskin,* Turner Sketches in the National Gallery, *1857, no. 70 (Library Edition, vol. XIII, 1904, p. 215); Finberg,* Turner Bequest, *1909, vol. II, p. 1020; Finberg,* Venice, *1930, p. 174.*

This was one of the "First Hundred" drawings selected by Ruskin from the Turner Bequest for public exhibition and can no longer be associated with any particular sketchbook; it is watermarked 1828. Its heavy rich colouring and the flat solid modelling of such forms as the gondola suggest that it was painted during the visit that Turner almost certainly made to Venice in 1835.

Ruskin suggests that this watercolour may have been inspired on returning from Torcello, on the opposite side of Venice from Fusina, and the sunset effect suggests that this is correct. He also writes of it: "The clouds are remarkable as an example of Turner's frequent practice of laying rich colour on a wet ground, and leaving it to graduate itself as it dried, a few subsequent touches being, in the present instance, added on the right hand [for another example see plate 5]. Although the boat in the centre seems a mere scrawl, the action of the gondolier (at the left-hand side) is perfectly given in his forward thrust." Turner's skill in suggesting a complex action by such simple means is all the more amazing in view of his inability to depict the human figure with any conviction on a large scale.

This watercolour is remarkable as an almost abstract essay in pure colour, arranged in three bands, the lowest, the lagoon, in no way reflecting the sunset tints of the sky. It seems to have been developed over the even simpler groundwork of a blue wash at the bottom, later painted over with green to represent water, and a pink one at the top, partly covered with the warm reds and yellows of the middle zone. Such lay-ins exist in some of Turner's sketchbooks (see the commentary on plate 9).

20 Storm at Venice

Probably 1835. Watercolour with pen and body-colour, $8^1/_2 \times 12^3/_8$ in. (21.6 × 31.5 cm.). *London, the British Museum (1915–3–13–50).*
COLLECTIONS: *William Quilter, sold at Christie's 8–10 April 1875 (240, as "Storm on the Lagunes"), bought by Agnew; the Rev. C. J. Sale, bequeathed to the British Museum 1915.*
LITERATURE: *Finberg*, Venice, *1930, p. 160.*

This watercolour is assigned by Finberg to Turner's Venetian visit of, almost certainly, 1835, a date that seems to be supported by its style and stormy subject. The gondola is drawn in flat washes like that on plate 17 and the line of buildings behind is more solidly modelled than comparable passages in the Venetian watercolours assigned to 1840 (see plate 24); the use of body-colour, even though this is here confined to two small areas, also differs from Turner's practice in 1840.

The composition with its diagonal stresses, here leading to the storm centre on the right, is also closer to works of the mid 1830s, such as the oil-painting of "The Burning of the Houses of Parliament" exhibited in 1835 and now at Cleveland, than to the more centralised vortex-like compositions of the 1840s (cf. for instance plate 25). In this watercolour the dramatic focus is accentuated by the silhouetting of the slanting black masts of the distant boats against the light and by the scratched-out line of surf, but the movement to the right is partly offset by the subsidiary centre of interest formed by the solid form of the gondola which moves towards the left and is placed under the strongest blues in the picture.

The stormy effect is further stressed by the menacing greyish-pink clouds, the two brilliantly white rents in the stormy sky, and the diffuse handling of part of the row of buildings on the left, seen as if through a scurry of rain. The form of the campanile, created by drawing a wide wet brush through the pigment, looms excitingly against the sky.

21 Lagoon Scene, Moonlight

Probably 1835. Watercolour, 7¹/₂×11 in. (19×27.9 cm.). *London, the British Museum (Turner Bequest CCCLXIV–334).*

EXHIBITED: Twee Eeuwen Engelsche Kunst, Stedelijk Museum, *Amsterdam, 1936 (237); J.M.W. Turner Watercolours, Tokyo and Osaka, 1963 (25, repr.), and Hong Kong, 1964 (25).*

LITERATURE: *Finberg*, Turner Bequest, *1909, vol. II, p. 1202.*

In its deep rich colouring and such details of handling as the flat modelling of the raft and the painting of some of the blues when the paper was wet, this is close to such works as "Venice from Fusina(?)", probably painted in 1835 (plate 19). Although the watercolour is listed by Finberg merely as "Lake view, Moonlight" some only partly legible lines in Turner's writing on the back refer to the moon and to Venice which "gleams its many winking lights".

The watercolour is a lesson in the subtle use of blues and blacks, resulting in a richness and variety that belies the restricted palette. The moon is shown by leaving the paper uncovered, its reflection by washing or scratching out.

CCCLXIV—334

22 Monte Rosa from the Val d'Aosta

Circa 1836. Watercolour, 9³/₈×11³/₄ in. (23.7×28.8 cm.). Cambridge, the Fitzwilliam Museum (1612). (Reproduced by permission of the Syndics of the Fitzwilliam Museum.)
COLLECTIONS: *W. G. Rawlinson by 1902; T. A. Tatton, sold at Christie's 14 December 1928 (27, as "In the Val d'Aosta"), bought by Lockett Thomson of Barbizon House, from whom bought by the Friends of the Fitzwilliam Museum 1932.*
EXHIBITED: *Whitechapel, 1953 (208);* The Romantic Movement, *Tate Gallery, 1959 (456, repr. pl. 51).*
LITERATURE: *Armstrong, 1902, p. 275; C. Lewis Hind,* Turner's Golden Visions, *1910, p. 199, repr. in colour facing p. 248; A. J. Finberg in* Barbizon House Record, *1932, no. 25, repr.; Finberg,* Life, *1939, pp. 360–1.*

Turner visited the Val d'Aosta during his first continental tour of 1802 and again in 1836 with his friend and patron H. A. J. Munro of Novar. This and a number of other watercolours, including two examples in the National Gallery of Scotland, one of them also of the Monte Rosa, presumably date from the time of the later visit. This visit also resulted in the oil-painting, now at Chicago, of "Snow-Storm, Avalanche, and Inundation – A Scene in the Upper Part of the Val d'Aout, Piedmont", which was bought by Munro at the Royal Academy in 1837.

Like the oil-painting this watercolour shows Turner's continuing interest in stormy scenes, but the treatment is broader than in the Venetian works of 1835, with a greater range and variation in tone of colour, and the effect is subordinated to a feeling of grandeur that harks back to the watercolours that resulted from Turner's first visit to Switzerland some thirty-five years earlier. But here the dwarfing of the small man-made structures by the towering mountains and heavy stormy sky no longer reflects the young artist's emulation of the Grand Manner and the Sublime but his own deep-felt sense of the littleness of man before the forces of nature.

23 A Gurnard

Circa 1839. Watercolour and touches of body–colour on grey paper, 7⁹/₁₆ × 10⁷/₈ in. (19.3 × 27.6 cm.). London, the Victoria and Albert Museum (P. 18–1938).
COLLECTIONS: *John Ruskin, bequeathed to Mr. and Mrs. Arthur Severn 1900; purchased at the Fine Arts Society 1900 by Robert Clarke Edwards, by whom bequeathed to the Victoria and Albert Museum 1918.*
EXHIBITED: *Ruskin's collection, Fine Art Society, 1878 (109, "Study for Fish") and 1900 (65, "Study for Fish").*
LITERATURE: *Ruskin*, Ruskin Collection, *1878 (Library Edition, vol. XIII, 1904, p. 469); T. S. R. Boase, "Shipwrecks in English Romantic Painting", in* Journal of the Warburg and Courtauld Institutes, *vol. XX, 1959, pp. 341–2.*

One of two similar sketches included in the 1878 and 1900 exhibitions of Ruskin's collection of drawings and watercolours by Turner. Ruskin's notes on the exhibition described them as studies "for the Slaver", the oil-painting of 1839 exhibited at the Royal Academy in 1840 as "Slavers throwing overboard the dead and dying — Typhon [*sic*] coming on"; the picture was given to Ruskin by his father in 1844 and is now at Boston. The gurnard in this drawing certainly resembles the fishes devouring the drowning slave in the foreground of the painting and stylistic reasons also suggest a date in the late 1830s. The handling is considerably looser than certain other drawings of fish such as that in the British Museum, Turner Bequest CCLXIII–339, dated circa 1815 by Finberg, and Turner's use of tinted paper is shown in its final stages, the rich and thickly-applied body-colour of *The Rivers of France* and Petworth drawings (see plates 12, 14 and 15), already more sparingly used in the works probably executed in Venice in 1835 (plates 17, 18 and 20), having now almost entirely disappeared.

Ruskin seems to have regarded his two drawings for the voracious fish of the "Slaver" as in some way embodying a criticism of contemporary life. Of this example he wrote "Looking up to the sky (modern philosophy?)" while its companion was described as "Coming on at speed... (modern trade?)". Turner's own intentions were, however, more directly concerned with the horrors of the slave trade, the picture being inspired by a passage in Thomson's *Seasons* and an account in Thomas Clarkson's *History of the Abolition of the Slave Trade*, first published in 1808 but re-issued in 1839, of how, in 1783, the captain of the slave-ship *Zong* threw his diseased slaves overboard because insurance could only be claimed for those "lost at sea", not for any dying through sickness.

24 Venice: the Giudecca from the Lagoon

Probably 1840. Watercolour, $8^{11}/_{16} \times 12^{5}/_{8}$ *in.* (22.1×32.1 cm.). *London, the British Museum (Turner Bequest CCCXV–12).*

EXHIBITED: *Huntington Library, San Marino, 1952;* Turner Watercolors, *Washington, Houston, San Francisco, Cleveland, Kansas City and Brooklyn, 1963–4 (59).*

LITERATURE: *Ruskin,* Turner Sketches in the National Gallery, *1857, no. 68 (Library Edition, vol. XIII, 1904, pp. 214–5); Finberg,* Turner Bequest, *1909, vol. II, p. 1017; Finberg,* Venice, *1930, pp. 122–31; Finberg,* Life, *1939, p. 381.*

Turner's last visit to Venice was in 1840; he went via Bregenz, where he was on the 10th or 11th August, and returned by way of Coburg, being there on the 17th or 20th September; he was back in London by the 7th October. This watercolour comes from a sketchbook almost certainly, for reasons of style, used on this visit. The handling is looser than in the watercolours ascribed to the 1835 visit, the colouring more varied and subtle. The forms are more ethereal, being suggested by tonal variations, assisted here and there by pen or brush-strokes, mainly in red, but also in blue and other colours. The foreground detail is less precise than that in the middle distance so that the eye is led into the depths of the centralised and, in the most gentle sense of the word, vortex-like composition.

Unlike the watercolours made on Turner's previous visits to Venice the compositions of some of those painted in 1840 were used, almost unchanged, for oil-paintings; another example from the same sketchbook (CCCXV–13) was echoed in "St. Benedetto, looking towards Fusina", exhibited in 1843, while the composition of Mr. David Ells' "The New Moon" was repeated in part of "The Dogano, San Giorgio, Citella, from the steps of the Europa", exhibited in 1842 (both oils are in the Tate Gallery). There is also less distinction between the watercolours and the very loose pencil sketches made on this visit; both are pictorial impressions rather than records.

25 Lyons

Circa 1840–5. Watercolour, $9^3/8 \times 11^7/8$ in. (23.8×30.2 cm.). *London, the Victoria and Albert Museum (977–1900).*

COLLECTIONS: *Henry Vaughan, by whom bequeathed to the Victoria and Albert Museum 1900.*

LITERATURE: *Armstrong, 1902, p. 265; Iolo A. Williams*, Early English Watercolours, *1952, repr. in colour as frontispiece.*

Turner had visited Lyons on his way to Italy in 1819 and 1828 but this watercolour appears to date from the early 1840s when, although Turner paid repeated visits to Switzerland, he seems usually to have travelled via the Low Countries and the Rhine. The depiction of figures and buildings by rapid drawing with the point of the brush, often in a completely unrealistic bright red, over flat washes which are themselves only slightly variegated in tone, is typical of his late technique, as is the subtle treatment of the sky in delicate superimposed washes.

The composition with its arched sky and deep recession to a central distant area of light, which is here accentuated by the pale streak drawn down through the washes of the sky to suggest the glare of the sun overhead, is also characteristic of many of Turner's works of the 1840s. Indeed, the cutting across of the corners by such forms as clouds and the bridge reflects a problem that worried him in many of the oils of this decade, leading in some cases to the actual avoidance of corners by the adoption of an octagonal format, as in "Shade and Darkness" and "Light and Colour" exhibited in 1843 (Tate Gallery). The problem was twofold, arising from Turner's growing use of compositions based on a deep funnel-like recession and from his realisation that the field of natural vision is eliptical rather than rectangular in form and becomes increasingly indeterminate at the edges.

26 Lake Scene, looking towards Mont Blanc from Geneva

Circa 1841–2. Watercolour and pen over pencil, $9^1/_{16} \times 11^1/_2$ in. (23.1×29.3 cm.).
London, the British Museum (Turner Bequest CCCXXXII–17).
LITERATURE: *Finberg*, Turner Bequest, *1909, vol. II, p. 1056.*

Turner had visited Geneva in 1802 and 1836, but this watercolour is one of a number of similar lake scenes possibly from a sketchbook containing other views of Lake Geneva, watermarked 1841 and presumably used during one of Turner's visits to Switzerland in 1841–4; another sketch possibly from this book, showing Bellinzona, was used for the watercolour painted in 1842-3 for H. A. J. Munro of Novar. The use of red pen-drawing to suggest detailed forms is typical of many of Turner's late watercolours, an analogous treatment being found in some of his oil-paintings, particularly the Venetian scenes exhibited between 1843 and 1846.

Turner's visits to Switzerland in 1841 and 1842 were the occasion of his trying to secure commissions, through his dealer Thomas Griffith, to make finished watercolours from his sketches. On each occasion he proposed to do ten subjects, but Griffith was only able to secure nine orders the first year and five the second, and even these were from three of his regular patrons, Munro, Ruskin and E. Bicknell.

27 Freiburg

Circa 1841–4. Pencil and watercolour, $9^1/_4 \times 13^3/_{16}$ in. (23.5×33.5 cm.). *London, the British Museum (Turner Bequest CCCXXXV–7).*

EXHIBITED: J.M.W. Turner Watercolours, *Tokyo and Osaka, 1963 (37, repr.), and Hong Kong, 1964 (37).*

LITERATURE: *Finberg,* Turner Bequest, *1909, vol. II, p. 1059, as "View of town".*

This is a page from a sketchbook used at Freiburg, South Germany, on the way to or from Switzerland, which Turner visited every year from 1841 to 1844; Finberg dates it about 1841.

In contrast to the more elaborate watercolours of the same period this is simply painted in broad washes of a few colours, fairly low in tone, floated over a slight pencil sketch. The texture of the paper has been used to break up the washes in the sky and to suggest the rising mists on the right. The foreground is the least clearly defined part of this impressionistic work which, unlike plates 26, 28 and 29, was never chosen for exhibition in the nineteenth century.

28 Ehrenbreitstein

EXHIBITED: Twee Eeuwen Engelsche Kunst, Stedelijk Museum, *Amsterdam*, *1936* *(238)*; L'Acquarelle Anglaise, *British Council, Geneva and Zürich*, *1955–6* *(129)*; The Romantic Movement, *Tate Gallery*, *1959* *(459)*; Turner Watercolors, *Washington, Houston, San Francisco, Cleveland, Kansas City and Brooklyn*, *1963–4* *(71)*.

LITERATURE: *Ruskin*, Turner Sketches in the National Gallery, *1857, no. 7 (Library Edition, vol. XIII, 1904, pp. 193–4)*; *Finberg*, Turner Bequest, *1909, vol. II, p. 1197*; *Clare, 1951, p. 106, repr. in colour facing p. 63*.

Turner first saw the great rock fortress of Ehrenbreitstein, opposite Coblenz, on his visit to the Rhine in 1817, and made a watercolour of it in 1819 for a projected series of *Tour of the Rhine* engravings (Bury Art Gallery, Lancashire). An oil-painting of the same subject was exhibited at the Royal Academy in 1835 (the Dowager Viscountess Allendale).

This view from Coblenz at sunset, sometimes known as the "pink" Ehrenbreitstein, is one of a number of studies of the fortress under different effects of light similar to those of the Rigi executed in 1842 to commissions arranged through Thomas Griffith. Though merely classified by Finberg among miscellaneous works in colour of from after about 1830, it can be shown to have come from a dismembered sketchbook, another page from which is watermarked with the date 1842, and therefore to have been the product of one of Turner's journeys to or from Switzerland between this date and his last visit in 1844. The irregular right-hand margin suggests that this work was torn out of a sketchbook and in fact it fits exactly with that of another watercolour of Ehrenbreitstein, showing almost the same view and effect of light, but less heavily worked (CCCLXIV–309). This in its turn is identical in style to the drawing watermarked 1842 (CCCLXIV–319) which stands in relation to a more finished "yellow" Ehrenbreitstein (CCCLXIV–346) much as its companion does to the work here illustrated.

This is a typical example of the varied techniques used by Turner in his later more finished watercolours. The delicate washes in the sky contrast with the way he treated the slope of the rock, where he worked the wet pink watercolour on the paper, added a heavier almost granular brown pigment, apparently with his fingers, and finally touched in a suggestion of detail with short strokes of pen or brush; he used similar short strokes to indicate the forms of the bridge of boats.

Circa 1842–4. Watercolour and pen, irregular, approx. $9^3/_4 \times 11^{15}/_{16}$ in. (24.8 × 30.3 cm.). London, the British Museum (Turner Bequest CCCLXIV–285).

74

29 Heidelberg

Probably 1844. Pencil and watercolour, 9¹/₁₆×12¹⁵/₁₆ in. (23×32.9 cm.). London, the British Museum (Turner Bequest CCCLII–17).

LITERATURE: ? *Ruskin*, Turner Sketches in the National Gallery, *1857, no. 84 (Library Edition, vol. XIII, 1904, p. 221); Ruskin*, Drawings and Sketches by Turner in the National Gallery, *1881, no. 49 (Library Edition, vol. XIII, 1904, p. 372); Finberg*, Turner Bequest, *1909, vol. II, p. 1161; Finberg*, Life, *1939, p. 402.*

The editors of the Library Edition of Ruskin's works identified this watercolour, under its earlier National Gallery number of 49, with number 84 in Ruskin's 1857 catalogue, but it is difficult to reconcile it with Ruskin's description. It may however have been one of the watercolours showing Heidelberg or described as being in the same sketchbook which were included in that catalogue, in particular numbers 11a, 16 or 18, which the Library Edition editors were unable to identify (vol. XIII, 1904, pp. 195, 197–8).

But the fact that Ruskin thought that the subject of his number 84 was a town in Eastern Switzerland does not rule out its identification with this watercolour, for in 1881 he listed what was definitely this work as "Baden (Swiss)"; even Finberg catalogued it as "Fribourg (?)". It is now recognised as a view of Heidelberg, seen across the river from the north with the castle on the left, and almost certainly comes from a sketchbook, watermarked 1844 and containing other watercolours of Heidelberg, made on Turner's return from his last visit to Switzerland in that year. There is a finished watercolour of Heidelberg in the Manchester City Art Gallery and an oil-painting in the Tate Gallery, but these were probably based on sketches made during previous visits to Germany.

This etherial watercolour, rather surprisingly chosen for exhibition at the National Gallery as early as 1857, is a fine example of Turner's floating of the thinnest of washes over the original pencil sketch (presumably made on the spot), so that both contribute equally to the final effect. With an extreme economy of means Turner uses only two basic colours, a blue, delicate but rich in hue, and a pale pinkish or yellowish brown.

CCCLII—17

30 Landscape
with a Mountain in the Middle Distance

Circa 1840–5 (?). Watercolour, 13×18⁷/₈ in. (33 × 48 cm.). *London, the British Museum (Turner Bequest CCLXIII–59).*
LITERATURE: *Finberg*, Turner Bequest, *1909, vol. II, p. 818.*

This watercolour is on paper watermarked 1828, but probably dates from considerably later. Although Turner paid his second visit to Italy in that year, spending about three months in Rome, the Italianate character of this sketch is no more specific than that in the many oil-paintings of Italian landscapes that Turner produced in his London studio during the next twenty years, and it is to the late never-exhibited examples of these that the watercolour shows most affinity. In its luminous washes of pale pink, blue and yellow it resembles such works, probably of about 1840 or later, as "Sunrise, Castle on a Bay" and "Norham Castle" (both in the Tate Gallery) in which Turner's use of oils came nearest to his watercolour technique. The unrealistic use of a strong red in the lower right-hand corner is also characteristic of his bold use of primary colours in his late works. Though classified by Finberg among a group of "colour beginnings" of circa 1820–30 this work may therefore be one of Turner's latest, and certainly most outstanding, creations.

31 Looking out to Sea: a Whale Aground

1845. Pencil and watercolour, 9⁵/₁₆×13³/₁₆ in. (23.7×33.5 cm.). *London, the British Museum (Turner Bequest CCCLVII–6).*

EXHIBITED: Turner Watercolors, *Washington, Houston, San Francisco, Cleveland, Kansas City and Brooklyn, 1963–4 (77).*

LITERATURE: *Finberg,* Turner Bequest, *1909, vol. II, p. 1167; Finberg,* Life, *1939, p. 408.*

This drawing comes from the Ambleteuse and Wimereux sketchbook, used on a brief visit to the French coast between Calais and Boulogne: three of the pages are dated the 12th May 1845 and the trip must have taken place between the 4th and 15th May, when Turner is recorded as having been in London.

The drawing seems to be inscribed, in Turner's nearly illegible hand, "I shall use this". Turner had two pictures of "Whalers" in the Royal Academy exhibition that had just opened and showed two more the following year (one of those exhibited in 1845 is at Washington; the others are in the Tate Gallery); the unexhibited "Sunrise with Sea Monster" (Tate Gallery) must also date from about this time. But the inspiration of the subject of the "Whalers" pictures was largely literary. Turner's encounter with a whale, if indeed this watercolour does represent an actual event, must be counted a lucky coincidence; the remaining sketches from the book, which includes several other coast scenes, show no more monsters. There are a number of sketches of whalers in action in the Whalers sketchbook of a few months earlier (British Museum, Turner Bequest CCCLIII), but these, though accompanied by studies of fish and the sea, are definitely works of imagination, not based directly on actual experience.

This is another example of the late Turner's economical use of a restricted range of delicate washes, but here much brighter colours are used than in the Heidelberg sketch of the previous year (plate 29). The splash of watercolour on the left, perhaps accidental, is cleverly used to suggest the splash of a breaking wave.

32 Eu with Louis Philippe's Château

1845. Pen and watercolour over pencil, 9¹/₁₆ × 12³/₄ in. (23 × 32.5 cm.). London, the British Museum (Turner Bequest CCCLIX–13).

EXHIBITED: ? *Laing Art Gallery, Newcastle, 1924 (151).*

LITERATURE: *Ruskin*, Turner's Sketches in the National Gallery, *1857, no. 4 (Library Edition, vol. XIII, 1904, p. 192); Redgrave*, A Century of British Painters, *1866, vol. II, pp. 86–7; Cook, 1905, p. 9, repr. p. 50; Finberg*, Turner Bequest, *1909, vol. II, p. 1169; Finberg*, Life, *1939, pp. 410–1.*

This watercolour is one of four similar views painted during Turner's second short visit to the French coast in 1845, to Dieppe and Picardy, which took place in September and early October; it was almost certainly originally part of the Eu and Tréport sketchbook, which was broken up and partly dispersed by Ruskin. This trip, when, according to the Redgraves, he was, "as he said himself, looking out for storms and shipwrecks", seems to have been the last he took abroad. It was also, according to the same source, the occasion of an unexpected invitation from King Louis Philippe, whom Turner had known many years earlier at Twickenham.

This is a more elaborate example of a watercolour made over a pencil sketch than the coast scene made earlier in the year (plate 31), but it shows the same use of bright colours, often completely unrealistic like the red cows, mauve buildings and brown horses and cart. These forms were broadly drawn with the brush while the redish-brown outlines of the trees in the middle distance on the right were drawn with a pen; scratching-out was used for the whites in the centre.

The abstract qualities of colour are also employed to create recession, alternating bands of brown, green, mauve, pink and pale brown leading back to the strongly marked blue of the distant sea, seen beyond the pink roofs of the château. The integrity of the surface is preserved by the light tones of both the foreground and the distant hills, together with the rising smoke or mist in the middle distance.

Acknowledgements:
All photographs are by Hans Hinz, Basel, with the exception of Plates 3, 9, and 14 which are by Zoltán Wegner, London.
The reproductions and offset-printing are by Imprimeries Réunies S. A., Lausanne.
The type used is 'Monotype'-Walbaum, and the text was printed by Verlagsanstalt Benziger & Co. AG., Einsiedeln.
The binding is by Max Grollimund, Basel.